The Amazing John Wesley

As you begin this journey remember: "Fear of the Lord is the beginning of wisdom: and the knowledge of the holy is understanding. Proverbs 9:10 KJV

Rev. Cynthia Willie Stewart, P.E
Eleventh Westchester District Conference
March 16, 2012

The Amazing

John Wesley

An Unusual Look at an Uncommon Life

H. NEWTON MALONY, PHD

Biblica Publishing
We welcome your questions and comments.

USA   1820 Jet Stream Drive, Colorado Springs, CO 80921
       www.authenticbooks.com
India Logos Bhavan, Medchal Road, Jeedimetla Village, Secunderabad
       500 055, A.P.

The Amazing John Wesley
ISBN-13: 978-1-60657-092-0

12 11 10 / 6 5 4 3 2 1

Published in 2010 by Biblica Publishing

A catalog record for this book is available through the Library of Congress.

Printed in the United States of America

Contents

Introduction

If there is only one event in the life of John Wesley that
people have heard about, it is probably the heartwarming
experience that changed his life. This occurred the night of May
24, 1738, during a prayer meeting sponsored by some Moravian
Christians. They were studying Martin Luther's comments on the
book of Romans. During the meeting Wesley had a religious experience. As Wesley heard such words as those of Romans 8:1, "There
is therefore now no condemnation for those who are in Christ
Jesus" (NRSV), he felt his heart strangely warmed and realized that
his sins were forgiven.

This was the experience that transformed Wesley's life and led
to over five decades of preaching the good news of the forgiveness
of sin across England, Wales, Scotland, and Ireland. The Wesleyan
movement has always been known as the "religion of the warm
heart" because of this experience of its founder.

Wesley told many of his friends that it was as if he had never
been a Christian before that night. He said at last he had experienced the inner witness of the heart that his father, Samuel, had

encouraged him to seek. It is strange that he mentioned this experience only once in the many sermons he subsequently preached. He did emphasize the importance of transforming, born-again experiences as he preached to the thousands who came to hear him. But he never focused on his own experience.

Why was Wesley so hesitant to talk about himself? Was it because some of his friends felt he was mentally ill to claim he was a new Christian? It was probably because he seemingly returned to being the Wesley he was before May 24, 1738, after the newness of the experience wore off. Wesley was a somewhat obsessive, highly compulsive, yet strangely timid person; and he incorporated the event into his long-established personal habits, behavioral tendencies, and religious style. After all, Wesley was born in 1703, and he was thirty-five years old when he accepted the invitation from his brother Charles to join him at the prayer meeting on that fateful night in May.

By this time Wesley

- had been an ordained priest in the Church of England for over a decade
- was a fellow of Lincoln College, Oxford, where he taught Greek and Hebrew
- had been one of the leaders of the Oxford Holy Club, where members had covenanted to meet daily in an effort to be serious Christians
- had joined others in weekly visits to the jail in Oxford, where he prayed with prisoners
- had written many letters to his mother, Suzanna, about his efforts to remain healthy by taking a cold swim in the Thames River every day and by not overeating
- had become a high-church Anglican who took the sacrament weekly and followed strict liturgy in worship

- had already published a book of hymns appropriate for church holy days
- had returned from North America, where he had been chaplain of Georgia for three years
- felt guilty over being unable to influence others to seriously study the Bible
- had lost the love of a young woman who married someone else when he had been too timid to propose
- had become depressed that he saved neither the Native Americans' souls or his own soul—two goals he had set for himself when he went to Georgia

All these religious experiences Wesley brought to that May prayer meeting on Aldersgate Street in London, and he would apply this wealth of skills and attitudes to how he would live after that event. These habits of study, self-discipline, social concern, intentionality, seriousness, alertness, and leadership colored everything he did to share his faith and apply those convictions to everyday life. Many of these post-Aldersgate activities and interests are less well-known aspects of Wesley's life, and they are the subjects of this book.

Before noting the specific ways he expressed his faith, other than through preaching, it is important to consider a general trait that characterized Wesley's whole personality. He was an *enthusiast*. His critics often used this label negatively to disparage the fact that he encouraged the expression of personal religious fervor outside the confines of traditional Anglicanism. He allowed nonrational sounds and body movements among those who were spiritually stirred by his preaching—which, incidentally, was done most often in the open air, outside church sanctuaries. When those who disliked Wesley called him an enthusiast, they usually meant *dangerous* enthusiast in the same way that many today label unfamiliar groups as dangerous cults. In fact, his detractors pointed out that one London hospital noted in its annual report that it had admitted a number of patients for mental illness and Methodism. They failed to note that Wesley cautioned his followers to be careful when they gave way to their emotions—although he never said that charismatic expressions were wrong.

Another meaning of the label *enthusiast* is more complimentary. When applied to Wesley, *enthusiast* means "eager," "open," "interested," "enthusiastic." Wesley was forever learning new things. His energy was indefatigable. He read widely and tried innovative ideas. He always carried books with him to read as he rode horseback from village to village. He arose every day at 4:00 a.m. and was energized well into the night. He kept a daily journal of the things that happened to him. As we shall see, this energetic curiosity led Wesley into novel areas that many would think unusual for a parish priest.

The first chapter, "John Wesley the Methodist," is a reprint of a tract Wesley wrote entitled *The Character of a Methodist*. He wrote this tract to counter the confusion and criticism that the movement had provoked. It is a statement of ideal Christian living as Wesley preached and taught it. Although written early in his outdoor preaching, much of what he wrote later simply elaborated these principles. It is amazing that he wrote this tract only three years after he began preaching outdoors. By this time he had adopted the label *Methodist* as the proper designation for the movement he had started. Previously, *Methodist* had been used only negatively to disparage an emphasis on living by schedules and rules.

The second chapter, entitled "John Wesley the Perfectionist," reflects the fact that Wesley was a child of the Enlightenment rather than the Reformation. He embraced the sixteenth-century reformers Calvin and Luther but went a step beyond their emphasis on God's power to save without any human effort other than faith. Wesley believed in the potential of human beings to change their lives. He believed that God intends for people to perfect their wholehearted love for him.

John Wesley was an organizer as well as a perfectionist. He conceived that each of the groups that responded to his preaching should be organized into classes that were to meet each week for accountability and spiritual growth. It is amazing that Wesley understood that decisions to follow Christ needed to be supported by social groups where people could meet together. These groups were the secret of Methodism's success. George Whitefield, the one who invited Wesley to preach outdoors, said he wished that he had organized his followers as Wesley did. Wesley's preaching had lasting results; Whitefield's did not.

The next chapter is entitled "John Wesley the Physician." Had *doctor* he not become a priest, John Wesley would probably have become a physician. He read widely in the medical field of his day. He was deeply concerned about the health of the poor, whom he felt were neglected by doctors who wanted reimbursement for their services. He wrote a health-care manual that went through thirty-six printings. It featured ingredients found in home kitchens. This book, *Primitive Physick: Or an Easy and Natural Method of Curing Most Diseases*, was the most popular book of its kind in Great Britain and North America well into the nineteenth century.

This chapter is followed by one entitled "John Wesley the Electrotherapist," which recounts the most unusual of the interests in which Wesley became involved—electricity. He heard about Benjamin Franklin's experiments and attended demonstrations of how static electricity could be transmitted from person to person. He became interested in how this could be used to help people who were sick. He set up hand-driven electrical machines in each of his free clinics and became known as one of the most outstanding electrotherapists of his generation. He wrote a book about electricity and saw it as a provision of God to relieve human suffering.

In the chapter "John Wesley the Spiritualist," the word *spiritual* is used in a unique sense. Wesley believed strongly in the spiritual realm. Unlike many educated people of his day, Wesley never gave up believing in the Devil. When he was a boy, a ghost called Old Jeffery haunted his childhood home for several months. Amazingly, Wesley analyzed this experience in detail and became intensely interested in other accounts of visitations and possessions. His journal describes many explorations into the stories people told him. He went out of his way on his travels to seek information on spirits.

John Wesley's romantic relationships are definitely not well known. Many people think he was a bachelor. However, Wesley was a romantic at heart. The chapter "John Wesley the Romantic" recounts four extended times in which he fell in love although he was timid and unsure of himself. At Oxford he wrote letters to a young woman he met at a friend's house. In Georgia he courted a Bible student. Later he pursued a fellow worker in the Methodist movement. Finally, he married a widow. It is amazing that none of these relationships was successful or brought happiness.

Perhaps the least known fact of Wesley's life is discussed in the chapter "John Wesley the Abolitionist." Wesley lived during the height of the North American slave trade. In Georgia he saw how cruel slavery could be. He wrote a book about it that became important to the abolitionist movement in England. In the last letter he wrote before his death in 1791, Wesley encouraged William Wilberforce in his desire to end slavery in the British empire. Wilberforce succeeded in 1810—almost two decades after Wesley's death.

Most know that Wesley kept a journal of his travels. However, the chapter "John Wesley the Writer and Publisher" details many more of his writings. Writing and publishing were probably the most amazing features of Wesley's life. While traveling on horseback thousands of miles and preaching over a thousand sermons each year, he wrote and published books, book abridgments, journals, and sermons; and he established libraries and founded a press. He even published a library of seventy books that he wanted placed in each of his chapels for followers to read. He said that "reading Christians are thinking Christians."

The last chapter, "John Wesley, a Man for All Reasons," discusses the meaning of Wesley's life for everyday Christian living. It has been said that John Wesley saved the British empire from the ravages of the French Revolution. He energized the faith and self-esteem of the lower classes in a manner that had not been done before. The Oxford Story, a long-standing tourist attraction in Oxford, England, presented Wesley as the most outstanding graduate of the university during the eighteenth century. Yet John Wesley was very human, as his life was replete with unfulfilled intentions, foibles, and mistakes in addition to monumental accomplishments. Wesley sincerely tried to base his whole life on the teachings of the Bible, and he cared deeply about the spiritual and physical lives of others. Christians can profit significantly from the lesser-known facts about Wesley's uncommon life that this book recounts.

1

Wesley the Methodist

This chapter is a reprint of a tract written by Wesley in 1741 and published in 1743 in London by John Goodin. Wesley wrote this just three years after he began field preaching. It is interesting that in this short time, the old label of "Methodist" that was applied negatively to Oxford's Holy Club when John and his brother Charles were its leaders, so quickly was embraced by Wesley as the positive label for his movement.

The content of this tract sets the themes for the rest of his ministry that ended with his death in 1791. The format of numbering the paragraphs is very typical of the way he wrote. The other label applied to the Oxford Holy Club was "Bible Bigots"—a label Wesley never used thereafter. However, it refers to the efforts of the Holy Club members to study and follow the teachings of the Bible. Wesley even said of himself, "I am a man of one book [the Bible]."

The Character of a Methodist

Not as though I had already attained[1]

TO THE READER

1. SINCE the name first came abroad into the world, many have been at a loss to know what a Methodist is; what are the principles and the practice of those who are commonly called by that name; and what are the distinguishing marks of this sect, "which is every-where spoken against."

2. And it being generally believed, that I was able to give the clearest account of these things, (as having been one of the first to whom that name was given, and the person by whom the rest were supposed to be directed,) I have been called upon, in all manner of ways, and with the utmost earnestness, so to do. I yield at last to the continued importunity both of friends and enemies; and do now give the clearest account I can, in the presence of the Lord and Judge of heaven and earth, of the principles and practice whereby those who are called Methodists are distinguished from other men.

3. I say those who are called Methodists; for, let it be well observed, that this is not a name which they take to themselves, but one fixed upon them by way of reproach, without their approbation or consent. It was first given to three or four young men at Oxford, by a student of Christ Church; either in allusion to the ancient sect of Physicians so called, from their teaching, that almost all diseases might be cured by a specific *method* of diet and exercise, or from their observing a more regular *method* of study and behaviour than was usual with those of their age and station.

4. I should rejoice (so little ambitious am I to be at the head of any sect or party) if the very name might never be mentioned more,

but be buried in eternal oblivion. But if that cannot be, at least let those who will use it, know the meaning of the word they use. Let us not always be fighting in the dark. Come, and let us look one another in the face. And perhaps some of you who hate what I am *called*, may love what I *am* by the grace of God; or rather, what "I follow after, if that I may apprehend that for which also I am apprehended of Christ Jesus."

The Character of a Methodist

1. THE distinguishing marks of a Methodist are not his opinions of any sort. His assenting to this or that scheme of religion, his embracing any particular set of notions, his espousing the judgment of one man or of another, are all quite wide of the point. Whosoever, therefore, imagines that a Methodist is a man of such or such an opinion, is grossly ignorant of the whole affair; he mistakes the truth totally. We believe, indeed, that "all Scripture is given by the inspiration of God;" and herein we are distinguished from Jews, Turks, and Infidels. We believe the written word of God to be the only and sufficient rule both of Christian faith and practice; and herein we are fundamentally distinguished from those of the Romish Church. We believe Christ to be the eternal, supreme God; and herein we are distinguished from the Socinians and Arians. But as to all opinions which do not strike at the root of Christianity, we think and let think. So that whatsoever they are, whether right or wrong, they are no distinguishing marks of a Methodist.

2. Neither are words or phrases of any sort. We do not place our religion, or any part of it, in being attached to any peculiar mode of speaking, any quaint or uncommon set of expressions. The most obvious, easy, common words, wherein our meaning can be conveyed, we prefer before others, both on ordinary occasions, and

when we speak of the things of God. We never, therefore, willingly or designedly, deviate from the most usual way of speaking; unless when we express scripture truths in scripture words, which, we presume, no Christian will condemn. Neither do we affect to use any particular expressions of Scripture more frequently than others, unless they are such as are more frequently used by the inspired writers themselves. So that it is as gross an error, to place the marks of a Methodist in his words, as in opinions of any sort.

3. Nor do we desire to be distinguished by actions, customs, or usages, of an indifferent nature. Our religion does not lie in doing what God has not enjoined, or abstaining from what he hath not forbidden. It does not lie in the form of our apparel, in the posture of our body, or the covering of our heads; nor yet in abstaining from marriage, or from meats and drinks, which are all good if received with thanksgiving. Therefore, neither will any man, who knows whereof he affirms, fix the mark of a Methodist here—in any actions or customs purely indifferent, undetermined by the word of God.

4. Nor, lastly, is he distinguished by laying the whole stress of religion on any single part of it. If you say, "Yes, he is; for he thinks 'we are saved by faith alone:'" I answer, You do not understand the terms. By salvation he means holiness of heart and life. And this he affirms to spring from true faith alone. Can even a nominal Christian deny it? Is this placing a part of religion for the whole? "Do we then make void the law through faith? God forbid! Yea, we establish the law." We do not place the whole of religion (as too many do, God knoweth) either in doing no harm, or in doing good, or in using the ordinances of God. No, not in all of them together; wherein we know by experience a man may labour many years, and at the end have no religion at all, no more than he had

at the beginning. Much less in any one of these; or, it may be, in a scrap of one of them: Like her who fancies herself a virtuous woman, only because she is not a prostitute; or him who dreams he is an honest man, merely because he does not rob or steal. May the Lord God of my fathers preserve me from such a poor, starved religion as this! Were this the mark of a Methodist, I would sooner choose to be a sincere Jew, Turk, or Pagan.

5. "What then is the mark? Who is a Methodist, according to your own account?" I answer: A Methodist is one who has "the love of God shed abroad in his heart by the Holy Ghost given unto him;" one who "loves the Lord his God with all his heart, and with all his soul, and with all his mind, and with all his strength.["] God is the joy of his heart, and the desire of his soul; which is constantly crying out, "Whom have I in heaven but thee? and there is none upon earth that I desire beside thee! My God and my all! Thou art the strength of my heart, and my portion for ever!"

6. He is therefore happy in God, yea, always happy, as having in him "a well of water springing up into everlasting life," and overflowing his soul with peace and joy. "Perfect love" having now "cast out fear," he "rejoices evermore." He "rejoices in the Lord always," even "in God his Saviour;" and in the Father, "through our Lord Jesus Christ, by whom he hath now received the atonement." "Having" found "redemption through his blood, the forgiveness of his sins," he cannot but rejoice, whenever he looks back on the horrible pit out of which he is delivered; when he sees "all his transgressions blotted out as a cloud, and his iniquities as a thick cloud." He cannot but rejoice, whenever he looks on the state wherein he now is; "being justified freely, and having peace with God through our Lord Jesus Christ." For "he that believeth, hath the witness" of this "in himself;" being now the son of God by faith. "Because he

is a son, God hath sent forth the Spirit of his Son into his heart, crying, Abba, Father!" And "the Spirit itself beareth witness with his spirit, that he is a child of God." He rejoiceth also, whenever he looks forward, "in hope of the glory that shall be revealed;" yea, this his joy is full, and all his bones cry out, "Blessed be the God and Father of our Lord Jesus Christ, who, according to his abundant mercy, hath begotten me again to a living hope—of an inheritance incorruptible, undefiled, and that fadeth not away, reserved in heaven for me!"

7. And he who hath this hope, thus "full of immortality, in every-thing giveth thanks;" as knowing that this (whatsoever it is) "is the will of God in Christ Jesus concerning him." From him, therefore, he cheerfully receives all, saying, "Good is the will of the Lord;" and whether the Lord giveth or taketh away, equally "blessing the name of the Lord." For he hath "learned, in whatsoever state he is, therewith to be content." He knoweth "both how to be abased and how to abound. Everywhere and in all things he is instructed both to be full and to be hungry, both to abound and suffer need." Whether in ease or pain, whether in sickness or health, whether in life or death, he giveth thanks from the ground of his heart to Him who orders it for good; knowing that as "every good gift cometh from above," so none but good can come from the Father of Lights, into whose hand he has wholly committed his body and soul, as into the hands of a faithful Creator. He is therefore "careful" (anxiously or uneasily) "for nothing;" as having "cast all his care on Him that careth for him," and "in all things" resting on him, after "making his request known to him with thanksgiving."

8. For indeed he "prays without ceasing." It is given him "always to pray, and not to faint." Not that he is always in the house of prayer; though he neglects no opportunity of being there. Neither

is he always on his knees, although he often is, or on his face, before the Lord his God. Nor yet is he always crying aloud to God, or calling upon him in words: For many times "the Spirit maketh intercession for him with groans that cannot be uttered." But at all times the language of his heart is this: "Thou brightness of the eternal glory, unto thee is my heart, though without a voice, and my silence speaketh unto thee." And this is true prayer, and this alone. But his heart is ever lifted up to God, at all times and in all places. In this he is never hindered, much less interrupted, by any person or thing. In retirement or company, in leisure, business, or conversation, his heart is ever with the Lord. Whether he lie down or rise up, God is in all his thoughts; he walks with God continually, having the loving eye of his mind still fixed upon him, and everywhere "seeing Him that is invisible."

9. And while he thus always exercises his love to God, by praying without ceasing, rejoicing evermore, and in everything giving thanks, this commandment is written in his heart, "That he who loveth God, love his brother also." And he accordingly loves his neighbour as himself; he loves every man as his own soul. His heart is full of love to all mankind, to every child of "the Father of the spirits of all flesh." That a man is not personally known to him, is no bar to his love; no, nor that he is known to be such as he approves not, that he repays hatred for his good-will. For he "loves his enemies;" yea, and the enemies of God, "the evil and the unthankful." And if it be not in his power to "do good to them that hate him," yet he ceases not to pray for them, though they continue to spurn his love, and still "despitefully use him and persecute him."

10. For he is "pure in heart." The love of God has purified his heart from all revengeful passions, from envy, malice, and wrath,

from every unkind temper or malign affection. It hath cleansed him from pride and haughtiness of spirit, whereof alone cometh contention. And he hath now "put on bowels of mercies, kindness, humbleness of mind, meekness, longsuffering:" So that he "forbears and forgives, if he had a quarrel against any; even as God in Christ hath forgiven him." And indeed all possible ground for contention, on his part, is utterly cut off. For none can take from him what he desires; seeing he "loves not the world, nor" any of "the things of the world;" being now "crucified to the world, and the world crucified to him;" being dead to all that is in the world, both to "the lust of the flesh, the lust of the eye, and the pride of life." For "all his desire is unto God, and to the remembrance of his name."

11. Agreeable to this his one desire, is the one design of his life, namely, "not to do his own will, but the will of Him that sent him." His one intention at all times and in all things is, not to please himself, but Him whom his soul loveth. He has a single eye. And because "his eye is single, his whole body is full of light." Indeed, where the loving eye of the soul is continually fixed upon God, there can be no darkness at all, "but the whole is light; as when the bright shining of a candle doth enlighten the house." God then reigns alone. All that is in the soul is holiness to the Lord. There is not a motion in his heart, but is according to his will. Every thought that arises points to Him, and is in obedience to the law of Christ.

12. And the tree is known by its fruits. For as he loves God, so he keeps his commandments; not only some, or most of them, but all, from the least to the greatest. He is not content to "keep the whole law, and offend in one point;" but has, in all points, "a conscience void of offence towards God and towards man." Whatever God

has forbidden, he avoids; whatever God hath enjoined, he doeth; and that whether it be little or great, hard or easy, joyous or grievous to the flesh. He "runs the way of God's commandments," now he hath set his heart at liberty. It is his glory so to do; it is his daily crown of rejoicing, "to do the will of God on earth, as it is done in heaven;" knowing it is the highest privilege of "the angels of God, of those that excel in strength, to fulfill his commandments, and hearken to the voice of his word."

13. All the commandments of God he accordingly keeps, and that with all his might. For his obedience is in proportion to his love, the source from whence it flows. And therefore, loving God with all his heart, he serves him with all his strength. He continually presents his soul and body a living sacrifice, holy, acceptable to God; entirely and without reserve devoting himself, all he has, and all he is, to his glory. All the talents he has received, he constantly employs according to his Master's will; every power and faculty of his soul, every member of his body. Once he "yielded" them "unto sin" and the devil, "as instruments of unrighteousness;" but now, "being alive from the dead, he yields" them all "as instruments of righteousness unto God."

14. By consequence, whatsoever he doeth, it is all to the glory of God. In all his employments of every kind, he not only aims at this, (which is implied in having a single eye,) but actually attains it. His business and refreshments, as well as his prayers, all serve this great end. Whether he sit in his house or walk by the way, whether he lie down or rise up, he is promoting, in all he speaks or does, the one business of his life; whether he put on his apparel, or labour, or eat and drink, or divert himself from too wasting labour, it all tends to advance the glory of God, by peace and good-will among men. His one invariable rule is this, "Whatsoever ye do, in

word or deed, do it all in the name of the Lord Jesus, giving thanks to God and the Father by him."

15. Nor do the customs of the world at all hinder his "running the race that is set before him." He knows that vice does not lose its nature, though it becomes ever so fashionable; and remembers, that "every man is to give an account of himself to God." He cannot, therefore, "follow" even "a multitude to do evil." He cannot "fare sumptuously every day," or "make provision for the flesh to fulfill the lusts thereof." He cannot "lay up treasures upon earth," any more than he can take fire into his bosom. He cannot "adorn himself," on any pretence, "with gold or costly apparel." He cannot join in or countenance any diversion which has the least tendency to vice of any kind. He cannot "speak evil" of his neighbour, any more than he can lie either for God or man. He cannot utter an unkind word of any one; for love keeps the door of his lips. He cannot speak "idle words;" "no corrupt communication" ever "comes out of his mouth," as is all that "which is" not "good to the use of edifying," not "fit to minister grace to the hearers." But "whatsoever things are pure, whatsoever things are lovely, whatsoever things are" justly "of good report," he thinks, and speaks, and acts, "adorning the Gospel of our Lord Jesus Christ in all things."

16. Lastly. As he has time, he "does good unto all men;" unto neighbours and strangers, friends and enemies: And that in every possible kind; not only to their bodies, by "feeding the hungry, clothing the naked, visiting those that are sick or in prison;" but much more does he labour to do good to their souls, as of the ability which God giveth; to awaken those that sleep in death; to bring those who are awakened to the atoning blood, that, "being justified by faith, they may have peace with God;" and to provoke those who have peace with God to abound more in love and in

good works. And he is willing to "spend and be spent herein," even "to be offered up on the sacrifice and service of their faith," so they may "all come unto the measure of the stature of the fullness of Christ."

17. These are the principles and practices of our sect; these are the marks of a true Methodist. By these alone do those who are in derision so called, desire to be distinguished from other men. If any man say, "Why, these are only the common fundamental principles of Christianity!" thou hast said; so I mean; this is the very truth; I know they are no other; and I would to God both thou and all men knew, that I, and all who follow my judgment, do vehemently refuse to be distinguished from other men, by any but the common principles of Christianity—the plain, old Christianity that I teach, renouncing and detesting all other marks of distinction. And whosoever is what I preach, (let him be called what he will, for names change not the nature of things,) he is a Christian, not in name only, but in heart and in life. He is inwardly and outwardly conformed to the will of God, as revealed in the written word. He thinks, speaks, and lives, according to the method laid down in the revelation of Jesus Christ. His soul is renewed after the image of God, in righteousness and in all true holiness. And having the mind that was in Christ, he so walks as Christ also walked.

18. By these marks, by these fruits of a living faith, do we labour to distinguish ourselves from the unbelieving world from all those whose minds or lives are not according to the Gospel of Christ. But from real Christians, of whatsoever denomination they be, we earnestly desire not to be distinguished at all, not from any who sincerely follow after what they know they have not yet attained. No: "Whosoever doeth the will of my Father which is in heaven, the same is my brother, and sister, and mother." And I

beseech you, brethren, by the mercies of God, that we be in no wise divided among ourselves. Is thy heart right, as my heart is with thine? I ask no farther question. If it be, give me thy hand. For opinions, or terms, let us not destroy the work of God. Dost thou love and serve God? It is enough. I give thee the right hand of fellowship. If there be any consolation in Christ, if any comfort of love, if any fellowship of the Spirit, if any bowels and mercies; let us strive together for the faith of the Gospel; walking worthy of the vocation wherewith we are called; with all lowliness and meekness, with long-suffering, forbearing one another in love, endeavouring to keep the unity of the Spirit in the bond of peace; remembering, there is one body, and one Spirit, even as we are called with one hope of our calling; "one Lord, one faith, one baptism; one God and Father of all, who is above all, and through all, and in you all."

2

John Wesley the Perfectionist

Wesley was not a perfectionist in the pathological sense of that label. Although he lived a highly scheduled life, he did not become emotionally disturbed or overly anxious when he failed to fulfill his goals or obstacles forced him to change his plans.

Yet in the religious sense of the term *perfectionist*, John Wesley was a prime example—more in what he taught than in what he claimed for himself. He took Jesus' admonition in Matthew 5:48—"Be perfect, therefore, as your heavenly Father is perfect" (NRSV)—utterly seriously, both as an ideal and as a possibility. This meant that Wesley believed that becoming a perfect Christian was possible here and now, before death, during a believer's lifetime. Perfection, or sanctification, became for Wesley the prime doctrine of Methodism. Very early in the movement, perfection was discussed and emphasized. Wesley noted, "The first tract I ever wrote expressly on this subject was published in the latter end of this year [1739].[1] That none might be prejudiced before they read it, I gave it the indifferent title of 'The Character of a Methodist.' In this I described a perfect Christian. . . . A Methodist is one who loves the Lord his God with all his heart, with all his soul, and with all his mind, and with all his strength."[2]

Yet Wesley's thinking about perfection had come much earlier—while he was a student at Oxford University in the mid-1720s. His reading of Jeremy Taylor's *Rules and Exercises for Holy Living and Holy Dying*, Thomas à Kempis's *The Imitation of Christ*, and William Law's *Christian Perfection: A Serious Call to the Devout and Holy Life* became the basis of the Holy Club—that group of students who covenanted to live dedicated Christian lives. The Holy Club was Wesley's first attempt to become perfect.

Perfection Defined

As time passed, perfection became the focus of the first ministerial conference held on June 25, 1744. You will notice in Wesley's account below that he had the habit of reporting discussions in the form of questions (Q) and answers (A).

Six clergymen and all of the preachers were present.[3]

The next morning we seriously considered the doctrine of sanctification, or perfection. The questions asked concerning it and the substance of the answers given were as follows:

Q: What is it to be *sanctified*?

A: To be renewed in the image of God, 'in righteousness and true holiness.'

Q: What is implied in being a *perfect Christian*?

A: The loving God with all our heart, and mind, and soul. (Deut. 6:5)

Q: Does this imply that *all* inward sin is taken away?

A: Undoubtedly; or how can we be said to be *saved from all our uncleannesses*? (Ezek. 36:29).[4]

The records of conferences in 1745–1747 continued the dialogue and show how central the doctrine of perfection had become. Wesley commented that everyone was in agreement by the end of the conferences and "whatever doubts anyone had when we met, they were all removed before we parted."[5] Although Wesley restated the doctrine several times throughout his life, he gave a succinct statement of his understanding of perfection at this time: "My brother and I maintained, (1) That Christian perfection is that love of God and our neighbour which implies deliverance from all sin. (2) That it is received merely by faith. (3) That it is given instantaneously, in one moment. (4) That we are to expect it, not at death, but every moment; that now is the accepted time, now is the day of salvation."[6]

Questions about Perfection

By the late 1750s this doctrine of perfection had engendered a significant amount of dissension and debate among Methodists and in the public at large. Concerns were several: (1) If believers are perfect, are they completely free from all sin? (2) Does perfection occur instantaneously or progressively (over months, years, or a lifetime)? (3) Is perfection possible this side of heaven? (4) Do believers know when they are perfect?

Of course, the debates about Wesley's perfectionism were not entirely new. While the response to his ideas at the June 1744 conference had been positive, the reaction to his sermon at Oxford's University Church of St. Mary two months later was so negative that the pulpits of the university became closed to him for the rest of his life. The clergy at Oxford were not receptive to Wesley's emphasis on the human struggle to reach perfection because they placed emphasis on God's power as the cause of perfection. In his preface to *Thoughts on Christian Perfection*, a tract Wesley published in 1759, he attempted to clarify his convictions without appearing contentious:

> The following tract is by no means designed to gratify the curiosity of any man. It is not intended to prove the doctrine at large, in opposition to those who explode and ridicule; no, nor to answer the numerous objections against it which may be raised by serious men. All I intend here is, simply to declare what are my sentiments on this head; what Christian perfection does, according to my apprehension, include, and what it does not; and to add a few practical observations and dimensions relative to the subject.

In this tract he showed a significant ability to tone down dogmatic assertions about sinlessness and treat objections to perfection more seriously.

First, he reiterated his contention that sinlessness does not mean freedom from ignorance, infirmities, or mistakes. Those who are perfect commit error when they do not know all they should know before they act. They commit error when they are sick, overwhelmed by the environment, or inadequate because of their own limitations. Perfect Christians make mistakes even when they are totally dedicated to God in mind, heart, and body. Yet Wesley admitted that there are times when mistakes do, indeed, violate the *ideal* will of God, and this is when those who are perfect have to rely on the redemptive work of Christ no less than when they were justified in the beginning of their Christian experience. This line of reasoning shows that Wesley was realistic in his thinking and reflection. Wesley observed, "I believe there is no such perfection in this life as excludes these involuntary transgressions, which I apprehend to be naturally consequent on the ignorance and mistakes inseparable from mortality. Therefore, *sinless perfection* is a phrase I never use, lest I should seem to contradict myself. I believe a person filled with the love of God is still liable to these involuntary transgressions. Such transgressions you may call sins, if you please: I do not."[7]

Next, Wesley considered whether perfection (i.e., death to sin, and renewal in love) occurs instantaneously or gradually. He opted for the latter in most cases. For the first time, Wesley used the phrase "grows in grace" to indicate that while believers may increasingly renounce sinful ways, they will be dead to sin only when they physically die. Interestingly, he contended that a Christian seeking perfection will continue to grow "in the knowledge of Christ, in his love and image of God; and will do so, not only till death, but to all eternity."[8]

Toward the end of the tract, Wesley answered the question of whether anyone ever achieved perfection before he or she died since Wesley had contended that most Christians did not. Wesley answered, "Convince me of this [i.e., that no one alive could reach perfection] and I will preach it no more. But understand me right; I do not build any doctrine on this or that person. . . . But if there are none made perfect yet, God has not sent me to preach perfection. . . . I believe some who died in this love enjoyed it long before their death. But I was not certain that their former testimony was true till some hours before they died."[9]

Certain aspects of this answer raise three issues that Wesley later addressed in *A Plain Account of Christian Perfection* (1777)—his most complete treatise on the subject. First, Wesley stated that he did not build the doctrine of perfection on this or that person. Then what was the basis of his reasoning? The answer is a doctrine of God and a doctrine of human beings. Second, Wesley implied that he had identified some who were perfect before death. Jane Cooper was such a person, and he told about her in the book.

Third, he referred to those who had claimed they were perfect and his uncertainty about the truth of their claims. In the book he referred to a tract (*To the Professors*) he wrote and a sermon ("The Nature of Enthusiasm") he delivered. In these writings he gave some cautionary advice to those who claimed they had reached perfection. Each of these issues is discussed below.

Wesley's Doctrines of God and of Human Beings

Wesley's doctrines of God and of human beings could be summed up in one word—*action*. Both God and human beings are active, that is, lively, dynamic, decisive, and forceful. The grace of God is not just something God did through Jesus' death. God's grace is an active force working in human hearts. According to Wesley, God's grace is like a seed planted in human beings. It is the power that leads them to seek God (prevenient grace); it is the power that saves them from sin (justifying grace); and it is the power that leads them to perfection (sanctifying grace).

Indeed, how God may work, we cannot tell; but the general manner wherein he does work is this: those who once trusted in themselves that they were righteous, that they were rich, and increased in goods, and had need of nothing, are, by the Spirit of God applying his word, convinced that they are poor and naked. All the things that they have done are brought to their remembrance and set in array before them; so that they see the wrath of God hanging over their heads, and feel that they deserve the damnation of hell. In their trouble, they cry unto the Lord, and he shows them that he hath taken away their sins, and opens the kingdom of heaven in their heart, 'righteousness, and peace, and joy in the Holy Ghost.' Sorrow and pain are fled away, and sin has no more dominion over them. Knowing they are justified freely through faith in his blood, they have peace with God through Jesus Christ.[10]

God for Wesley is very active, assertive, and convincing in leading persons into an awareness of their need of him (prevenient grace) and in convincing them of his love and forgiveness (justifying grace). God continues to work in their lives and lead them toward perfection (sanctifying grace). As Wesley stated, "A perfect man, is one in whom God hath fulfilled his faithful word. . . . We understand hereby one whom God hath 'sanctified throughout in body, soul, and spirit;' one who 'walks in the light as He is in the light; in whom is no darkness at all, the blood of Jesus Christ his Son having cleansed him from all sin.'"[11]

It is important to realize that this view of God differed considerably from that of the Protestant Reformers. Wesley knew well and appreciated Luther and Calvin—both of whom lived in the 1500s. But he disagreed strongly with Calvin's doctrine of predestination and Luther's doctrine of justification. He said he could not with a clear conscience call people to salvation all over the British Isles and Ireland if he believed God had already chosen whom he would save and whom he would damn (predestination). Further, he did not believe God's grace is simply a new way God looked at people after Jesus' crucifixion or that human beings remain sinners until they die (justification without the possibility of sanctification). For Wesley, in addition to saving humans for heaven, God is at work here and now, restoring the world to his righteous will. And this understanding of God's grace is different from that of the Reformers.[12]

Wesley's active view of God was paralleled by a similar view of the human being. Wesley was a child of the Enlightenment.

The two hundred years following the late Middle Ages, in which Calvin and Luther lived, saw the rise of human ingenuity and power. Wesley reflected this in his understanding of the ability of the human to achieve perfection. Faith is not simply the acceptance of salvation, as in Luther's concept of salvation by faith alone. Nor is faith some sense of having been chosen by God, as in Calvin's concept of predestination, with no requirement of good works. Wesley's alternative can be seen in the following:

Q22: By what 'fruit of the Spirit' may we 'know that we are of God,' even in the highest sense?
A. By love, joy, peace, always abiding by invariable long-suffering, patience, resignation; by gentleness, triumphing over all provocation; by goodness, mildness, sweetness, tenderness of spirit; by fidelity, simplicity, godly sincerity; by meekness, calmness, evenness of spirit; by temperance, not only in food and sleep, but in all things natural and spiritual.

Q23: But what great matter is there in this? Have we not all this when we are justified?
A. What, total resignation to the will of God, without any mixture of self-will, gentleness, without any touch of anger, even the moment we are provoked? Love to God, without the least love to the creature, but in and for God, excluding all pride? Love to man, excluding all envy, all jealousy, and rash judging? Meekness, keeping the whole soul inviolably calm? And temperance in all things? Deny that any ever came to this, if you please; but do not say all who are justified do.[13]

According to Wesley, humans are active and self-determining. They can grow in grace and fall from grace. He stated:

It is otherwise with the generality of those that are justified; they feel in themselves more or less pride, anger, self-will, a heart bent to backsliding. And, till they have gradually mortified these, they are not fully renewed in love.

Q25: But is not this the case of all who are justified? Do they not gradually die to sin and grow in grace, till, or perhaps a little before death, God perfects them in love?

A: I believe this is the case of most, but not all. God usually gives a considerable time for men to receive light, to grow in grace, to do and suffer his will, before they are either justified or sanctified; but he does not invariably adhere to this; sometimes he 'cuts short his work;' he does the work of many years in a few weeks; perhaps in a week, a day, an hour.[14]

Here we can see a vibrant combination of Wesley's active view of God and human beings.

Jane Cooper: Perfection before Death

While Wesley held on tenaciously to the conviction that perfection was possible before death, the only example he ever gave of this in writing was that of Jane Cooper. He stated, "In the latter end of this year [1761], God called to himself that burning and shining light, Jane Cooper. As she was both a living and a dying witness of Christian perfection, it will not be at all foreign to the subject to add a short account of her death; with one of her own letters, containing a plain and artless relation of the manner wherein it pleased God to work 'that great change in her soul.'"[15]

We are not told how old Jane Cooper was when she died or when she first became a Christian. The long letter from her to

Wesley that he reprinted in his book is dated May 2, 1761. The beginning of her letter implies she was already sick with smallpox. She apparently lived near London because she mentioned going to hear Wesley preach and returning as she struggled to attain some inner peace early in her Christian experience. She confessed, "I was in a moment enabled to lay hold on Jesus Christ, and found salvation by simple faith."[16] Her letter continues with an affirmation of her growth in her faith.

> I saw Jesus altogether lovely; and knew he was mine in all his offices. And, glory be to him, he now reigns in my heart without a rival. I find no will but his. I feel no pride; nor any affection but what is placed on him. I know it is by faith I stand; and that watching unto prayer must be the guard of faith. I am happy in God this moment, and I believe for the next. . . . I desire to be lost in that 'love that passeth understanding.' I see the 'just shall live by faith;' and unto me, who am less than the least of all saints, is this grace given. If I were an archangel, I should veil my face before him, and let silence speak his praise.[17]

In November 1761, Wesley commented that Jane sent a note to him indicating she knew she was going to die. She wrote, "I suffer the will of Jesus. All he sends is sweetness by his love. . . . I cannot be frightened by his will."[18] On the Friday before she died, Wesley came to see her. She said, "Sir, I did not know that I would live to see you." He asked her, "Do you now believe you are saved from sin?" She answered, "Yes, I have had no doubt of it for many months. That I ever had, was because I did not abide in the faith. I now feel I have kept the faith; and perfect love casts out fear. . . . I have been a great enthusiast, as they term it, these six months; but never lived so near the heart of Christ in my life."[19] She died three days later after fifteen hours of intense suffering.

It is noteworthy that Wesley's only account of a living person who had attained perfection was someone so near death. Although he asserted that perfection this side of death is possible, he was very cautious in identifying anyone as perfect. It is interesting that Jane Cooper claimed in her last statement to be an "enthusiast" and that Wesley made no comment on her claim. As can be seen in the following section, he was usually somewhat critical of those whose behavior was labeled "enthusiastic."

Enthusiasm and Perfection

In Wesley's book *A Plain Account of Christian Perfection*, this account of Jane Cooper's experience follows a lengthy question-and-answer section that Wesley wrote in response to a flurry of people who asserted they had achieved perfection. Some of them were "enthusiasts"—a term applied to those who expressed strong emotions and made extravagant claims.

The Methodist movement was often accused of *enthusiasm*—defined as becoming hyperemotional rather than rationally dogmatic in religion. In a manner similar to current charismatic religious expressions, a number of individuals during Wesley's life-time claimed they had become possessed by the Holy Spirit to the point where they had special knowledge and privilege. Foretelling of the future, speaking in tongues, unusual healings, possessions of various types, groans, barks, dancing, and so forth occurred—all related to the doctrine of perfection. One mental hospital in London claimed that it had admitted over ninety patients during the last year for madness and Methodism.

Wesley maintained his conviction about the possibility of sanctification, yet he was very ambivalent about the ways it should be expressed. He was a child of his age and was convinced that reason, not feeling, should guide faith. In regard to the flourish of new converts in London in 1762, Wesley confessed his dilemma:

> Easily foreseeing that Satan would be endeavouring to sow tares among the wheat, I took much pains to apprise them of the danger, particularly with regard to pride and enthusiasm. And while I stayed in town, I had reason to hope they continued both humble and sober-minded. But almost as soon as I was gone, enthusiasm broke in. Two or three began to take their own imagination for impressions from God, and thence to suppose they should never die; and these, labouring to bring others into the same opinion, occasioned much noise and confusion. Soon after, the same persons, with a few more ran into other extravagances; fancying that they could not be tempted; that they should feel no more pain, and that they had the gift of prophecy, and of discerning of spirits. At my return to London, in autumn, some of them stood reproved; but others were got above instruction. Meantime, a flood of reproach came upon me almost from every quarter; from themselves, because I was checking them on all occasions; and from others, because, they said, I did not check them.[20]

This led to the great increase of the number and courage of those who opposed perfection, according to Wesley. He preached his sermons "On the Nature of Enthusiasm" and wrote his tract *Cautions and Directions Given to the Greatest Professors in the Methodist Societies* (those who claimed to be perfect). He also preached a sermon on "The More Excellent Way" about the gifts of the Holy Spirit.[21]

Wesley felt that the chief danger of enthusiasm was pride. He warned, "Watch and pray continually against pride. . . . You may slide back into it unawares. For it is pride, not only to ascribe anything we have to ourselves, but to think we have what we really have not. Mr. L., for instance, ascribed all the light he had to God, and so far he was humble; but then he thought he had more light than any man living; and this was palpable pride . . . or if you think you are so taught of God, as no longer to need man's teaching; pride lieth at the door."[22]

Wesley also advised against antinomianism—the belief that love superseded the law and that those who were perfect no longer had any reason to attend services or follow rules. Sangster recounted the experience of John Nelson, a helper of Wesley, who often encountered those who raved about what they called "happy-sinnership." Nelson met a fellow who was so drunk that he could hardly stand. Nelson "asked him what he thought of himself now, if death were to seize him in that wretched condition. He said, that 'he was not afraid to die, for he was as his Saviour would have him to be, and if He would have him to be whole, He would make him so; but he was a poor sinner and he hoped to be so in eternity. You and John Wesley are enemies of the Lamb, for you want people to be holy here. But the Lamb of God shall have the honour of saving me; I will not offer to save myself, like you Pharisees.'"[23]

Wesley cautioned against thinking that we can become so filled with love that we need not continue to pursue holiness. Some who claimed perfection were irregular in attendance at meetings of the Societies. They claimed they were above the law and were self-indulgent. Wesley cautioned against no longer searching the Scriptures or claiming that all an individual has to do is believe. Further, he warned against stillness—the tendency to desist from good works and believe that faith alone is sufficient for salvation—the Lutheran heresy, according to Wesley.

While Wesley agreed with the Reformers in denying "works righteousness," he yet cautioned the enthusiasts to resist sins of omission. He wrote, "Be zealous of good works; willingly omit no work, either of piety or mercy. . . . Be active. Give no place for indolence or sloth; give no occasion to say, 'Ye are idle, ye are idle.' . . . Be always employed; lose no shred of time, gather up the fragments, that nothing be lost. And whatsoever thy hand findeth to do, do it with thy might."[24]

Interestingly, Wesley advised against too much talk: "Be slow to speak and wary in speaking. . . . Do not talk much, neither long at a time."[25] He felt the enthusiasts were prone to claim too much, provoke schism, and criticize preachers; and they were pompous in their claims and often sought approval. He observed that growing in grace tended to have built-in dangers of this sort. Wesley advised, "Beware of impatience or contradiction. Do not condemn, or think hardly of those who cannot see as you see, or who judge it their duty to contradict you, whether in a great thing or small. . . . O beware of touchiness, of testiness, not bearing to be spoken to. . . . Expect contradiction and opposition, together with crosses of various kinds."[26]

Finally, Wesley cautioned against enthusiasm itself. "Beware of that daughter of pride, enthusiasm. O keep at the utmost distance from it! Give no place to a heated imagination. Do not hastily ascribe things to God. Do not easily suppose dreams, voices, impression, vision, or revelations, to be from God. They may be from him. They may be from nature. They may be from the devil. . . .You are in danger of enthusiasm every hour, if you depart ever so little from Scripture; yes, or from the plain, literal meaning of any text, taken in connection with the context."[27]

In contrast to all these erroneous manifestations of perfection, Wesley, in his sermon "The More Excellent Way," urged his followers to covet earnestly the best gifts (1 Corinthians 12:31) and emphasized that true perfection would be seen in those who evidenced the "fruit of the [Holy] Spirit . . . love, joy, peace, patience, kindness, generosity, faithfulness, gentleness, and self-control" (Galatians 5:22–23 NRSV).

Conclusion

As noted earlier, Wesley believed perfection to be the cardinal doctrine of Methodism. He never wavered in this conviction. Early in his book *A Plain Account of Christian Perfection* he claimed that perfection was the same doctrine that he and his brother Charles had affirmed from 1725 to 1777—the date of the book's publication. He concluded his book with these words, "And this is the whole and sole perfection, as a train of writings prove to a demonstration, which I have believed and taught these forty years."[28] He instructed his preachers to "make a point of preaching perfection to believers constantly, strongly and explicitly, and all believers should mind this one thing, and continually agonize for it."[29]

3

John Wesley the Organizer

Wesley's religious experience at Aldersgate set his mind to work on how to share his zeal with everyone he met. But it did not prepare him for the excitement he felt after joining his close friend George Whitefield for an open-air preaching service in Bristol's Kingswood slums in late March 1739. Worship outside the walls of a church was unheard of. But Wesley found himself deeply moved by the energetic outdoor response of these folk who would rarely darken the doors of a parish church. His journal reflects his feelings: "In the evening I reached Bristol, and met Mr. Whitefield there. I could scarcely reconcile myself at first to this strange new way of preaching in the fields, of which he set me an example on Sunday; having been all my life (till very recently) so tenacious of every point relating to decency and order, that I should have thought the saving of souls almost a sin if it had not been done at church."[1]

Although this venue was new, the popularity of George Whitefield was well known. Whitefield was a twenty-three-year-old cleric who had been a member of Wesley's Holy Club at

Oxford. His compelling preaching had captivated large crowds in the churches of London. Many times those who came to hear him filled the sanctuaries and spilled over into surrounding streets. He could have been called the Billy Graham of his day. The lively response to his preaching aroused some jealousy among the parish clergy, however. They were somewhat relieved when Whitefield announced that he, like his friends John and Charles Wesley, had decided to go to Georgia as an evangelist.

Whitefield had been in Georgia for only a few months when he decided to return to England to raise money for a new venture—the building of an orphanage to house the many children whose families had been devastated by frequent epidemics in North America. Whitefield hoped that his popularity as a preacher would open church doors to his appeal for the necessary funds. He was stunned to realize, however, that during his absence many pastors had adopted a negative reaction to his ministry. Copying the success of the Welch layman Howell Harris in preaching outdoors, Whitefield decided to try this method of evangelism and fund-raising. On February 17, 1739, he preached his first outdoor sermon to an audience of about two hundred in Bristol's Kingswood slums—one of the vilest domains in all of England and the home of coal miners.

In the next few weeks as many as twenty thousand miners came out to hear Whitefield preach. Encouraged by this response, he extended his preaching to sites all over Bristol. Even the wealthy came to hear him. Funds for his orphanage came in, and Whitefield made plans to return to North America. He began to look for a successor to his field preaching and thought of his friend John Wesley—his mentor at Oxford, ten years his senior. Whitefield was so sure of Wesley's accepting the invitation that he announced Wesley's coming in the Bristol newspaper.

Wesley, however, was not so confident that replacing Whitefield was the right thing for him to do. He struggled with the decision, and, finally, he cast lots. The lot said "Bristol."

The morning of April 1, 1739, Whitefield preached his last sermon in the fields. That same day, in the afternoon, Wesley preached for the first time in the open air. Wesley's journal account reads: "At four in the afternoon, I submitted to be more vile, and proclaimed in the highways the glad tidings of salvation, speaking from a little eminence in the ground adjoining to the city to about three thousand people."[2]

Henderson (1997) summarized the import of these two events: "Whitefield had initiated and popularized mass evangelism to the unchurched, but Wesley *organized* the movement and brought it under systematic management"[3] (italics mine). Wesley accomplished what Whitefield did not—he organized the responses to his preaching into a cohesive movement. Adam Clarke, an early historian of Methodism, recorded an encounter where Whitefield complimented Wesley for his organizational skills and bemoaned the fact that he had not made any effort to bring his converts together in any group. Whitefield's response to a man who said he was a Wesleyan was, "Thou art in the right place. My brother Wesley acted wisely—the souls that were awakened under his ministry he joined in class, and thus preserved the fruits of his labor. This I neglected, and my people are a rope of sand."[4]

Wesley's organization is known as the Class Meeting. However, the Class Meeting was only one of five interlocking groups Wesley planned for responders to his preaching. These five groups were the following:

1. *Society*—an assembly of all interested persons
2. *Class Meeting*—a small group of ten to twelve members trying to follow Christ in their day-to-day behavior

3. *Band*—an even smaller group of people desiring to deepen their spirituality

4. *Select Society*—an elite corps of those training to be leaders

5. *Penitent Band*—a group for those trying to overcome all their sinful habits and go on to perfection

Before discussing each of these in more detail, it is important to consider the origins of Wesley's organizational thinking.

Childhood Training

Labeling the Wesleyan movement *Methodist* was not done casually or arbitrarily. Living by a method characterized Wesley's total life. It could be said to have originated in his childhood. His father, Samuel, spent time instructing all of his children in classical languages. Several of the children could read the Greek New Testament by the time they were ten years old. Suzanna, his mother, organized the rearing of her children into regular hours of study and assigned chores for every day. In addition to this daily schedule, she planned to spend at least an hour a week with each of her nine children who lived into adolescence. John's day was Thursday. In later years she wrote a description of her method in response to John's request. He published her description in the *Arminian Magazine*. Here she stated a theme that was to become a dominant feature in Wesley's groups—namely, the conquest of the *will*. Suzanna believed that becoming an adult involved redirecting the child's will to the authority of the parent. John believed that becoming a Christian involved redirecting the individual's will to the authority of God. None of the children ever expressed (in writing, at least) anything other than appreciation for the way she organized their upbringing.

As a student at Oxford, John wrote his mother about how he was living by a similar daily schedule that included exercise, dieting, swimming in the Thames River, and drinking a certain amount of cold water. He even recommended that she, too, adopt the teachings of a doctor from Bath who had cured himself of obesity by self-control.

The Holy Club

The clearest example of the type of organization that later characterized Wesley's groups can be seen in the Oxford University Holy Club, of which John became the leader. Charles, John's younger brother, had founded the club while John was away serving as curate under his father's direction. The term *Methodist* was first applied to this Oxford group. Members of the group committed themselves to living by a strict schedule—that is, a method. They met daily after supper for worship and to reflect on their Christian witness during the day. They read the Bible, prayed, visited the sick and imprisoned, witnessed to their faith, performed deeds of loving-kindness, sought to let God guide them in every way, and took Holy Communion together at least once a week.

Although the Holy Club evoked much attention on the Oxford campus, such an organization was not entirely unique in eighteenth-century Anglicanism. Over a half century earlier, religious societies had been organized by Dr. Anton Horneck as a means by which young men could meet together in pursuit of the Christian life. While such societies were rare at Oxford, they were, no doubt, well known to the Wesley brothers and their friends.

Two aspects of the Holy Club can be seen in the five groups that later characterized the Wesleyan movement. First, the Holy Club emphasized group experience. Wesley was intuitively a good social psychologist. He sensed the power of social support and interpersonal association. Although Whitefield assumed that people need only to make a decision to accept Christ in order to be a Christian, Wesley realized that Christians need the support of others who share their commitment and to whom they can be responsible.

Second, the Holy Club emphasized behavior over personal experience. Although this emphasis on behavior later came to haunt him in that it took a "heartwarming experience" to convince him of his own salvation, the Holy Club was essentially an action-oriented, good-deed, behavior-focused method of Christian living. Wesley later clearly wrote against mysticism and quietism—those forms of Christianity that focused on personal devotion and solitary waiting on God to act. He fully agreed with James's contention that "faith by itself, if it has no works, is dead" (James 2:17 NRSV).

The Congregation in Savannah

Soon after arriving in Georgia, Wesley attempted to organize some semblance of the Holy Club within the parish at Savannah. He divided the total church membership into smaller groups and had them meet regularly for teaching and sharing. He selected a small group called "faithful men" with whom he met on Sunday afternoons for more concentrated spiritual development. He called these groups "little societies" and described the structure of these groups in his journal: "To select out of these [the congregation] a smaller number for a more intimate union with each other which might be forwarded, partly by our conversing single with each, and partly by inviting them all together in our house: and this, accordingly, we determined to do every Sunday in the afternoon."[5]

This was the first application of the Holy Club model to a whole congregation. Previously, such groups had simply been voluntary groups rather than a requirement for all members of a parish. Wesley felt that every church member should grow and develop in Christian living—not just a few. Such an expectation has met two problems from that day to this: how to get everyone involved and how to meet different levels of experience, motivation, and intelligence.

The Fetter Lane Society

Even before his Aldersgate experience, Wesley was one of the leaders in the Fetter Lane Society (note the label "Society")—a group of about forty persons who met for prayer and encouragement every Wednesday night in London. Although it was patterned on the Anglican Religious Society model, its form and method were greatly influenced by the Moravians—the German pietistic group that influenced Wesley during a storm on his trip to Georgia. It was in a Moravian prayer meeting on Aldersgate Street that Wesley had his salvation experience. The Moravians had fellowship groups called bands—a term Wesley later adopted for the Methodist movement.

In the Fetter Lane Society, thirty-three articles defining admission, functioning, cohesion, and expulsion were drawn up by Wesley and Peter Bohler, a Moravian leader. Henderson pointed out that these rules dealt almost entirely with the procedure—not the content—of the meetings.[6] Such rules as ending time, confidentiality, and standing to speak were detailed. The group met every Wednesday evening for instruction and answering questions of self-examination. Every member was expected to report about his or her own spiritual condition, and all members were expected to listen and respond to one another. Wesley envisioned this structure to be a reinstatement of the order of the early Christian church. For Wesley the Fetter Lane Society became the center of his ministry during the two years before he began to preach in

Bristol. However, as his fame as a preacher spread, his attendance became more sporadic, and his control of the method of the Society became more problematic—a problem that was to plague the structure he imposed on his groups that formed in response to his travels.

Transformations in Bristol and London

In Bristol Wesley transformed already-existing Anglican Societies and added Band meetings of a type that were in effect in the Fetter Lane Society. He realized that he was ministering to a nonchurch type of person with whom he had not been associated before. His motto was "To spread scriptural holiness throughout the land." Henderson stated well how Wesley adapted the gentleman's world of Oxford to his working-class audience: "Wesley took his appeal to the common people of England, and on their own turf and in their own terminology."[7] He expounded in regular Society meetings on various aspects of Christian behavior and organized members in Bands, where members followed the early church described in the book of Acts by giving weekly accounts of their spiritual progress. Wesley was very clear in what he called "his design" to "provide plain truth for plain people . . . [to] abstain from all nice and philosophical reasoning . . . [and to avoid] those modes of speaking which men of reading are acquainted with, but which to common people are an unknown tongue."[8]

There is a tendency to presume that Wesley's preaching in the open air in Bristol led him to embark immediately on a preaching tour all over England with a fully developed group model in hand. This was not true, although the seeds of his later journeying were certainly present. As a matter of fact, he went back and forth from Bristol to London for the next several years. As with Whitefield, the enthusiastic response to Wesley's field preaching led to the disapproval of the Church of England and the reluctance of priests to open their pulpits to him.

A place for meetings was needed. In November 1739 Wesley agreed to purchase an old foundery on City Road near Moorfields in London. The foundery was redecorated to include an auditorium where over three hundred people could meet to rethink his group methods.[9] Wesley established a new group called the *United Society* with a set of rules that became the model for the Methodist movement from that time on. He had been influenced by both the mission Societies of the Church of England and the bands of the Moravians. The United Society was a hybrid of both of these with some uniquely Wesleyan additions. Wesley announced an open admission policy for people anywhere who had a "desire to flee from the wrath to come, to be saved from their sins."[10] To control those who were backsliders or who were not serious in their participation, members were reevaluated by Band members and issued tickets for three months at a time. New members were issued tickets for a two-month trial period. Wesley appointed "stewards" to take care of financial matters, "sick visitors" to visit the infirmed, and "lay assistants" to expound the Scriptures. The United Society became the title Wesley used for every group organized after his preaching in the British Isles. It should be noted that he did not call these groups "churches." This change only came later.

The United Society at the Foundery in London grew to over nine hundred by 1741, and similar Societies were formed in Bristol, the Midlands, and even farther north. Out of a concern for better supervision coupled with a need for more systematic financial support, Wesley approved the suggestion that each Society be organized into groups whose members would agree to give a penny a week for supporting the cause. And so the well-known *Methodist Class Meeting* was born. In part, these groups were a revival of what Wesley had attempted, with only minimal success, in the parish in Georgia. But here it became a requirement for Society membership and included lay oversight for commitment, health, and financial offering for the poor. Each Class leader was to have weekly contact with all Class members and inform the minister of any special needs.

Wesley added to this structure a *Select Society* for those who most seriously committed to spiritual development and a *Penitent Band* for those needing rehabilitation from severe moral and social problems.

So the framework was laid for the interlocking five-group structure of the Wesleyan movement in the eighteenth century, which will be discussed in more detail in the section to follow. Each of the five groups used a different mode of interacting in order to meet a different need. The Society used a cognitive mode of interaction; the Class Meeting, a behavioral mode; the Band, an affective mode; the Select Society, a training mode; and the Penitent Band, a rehabilitative mode.

The Society

The Society is similar to what we would call the congregation. Initially, it was composed of those who wanted to listen to Wesley's preaching. It came to include all interested persons. Later, after the Methodist movement got under way, it was the gathering where Wesley preached on his travels. At Society meetings, which occurred on Sunday nights, sermons were preached, Christian living was explained, Scriptures were interpreted, and the movement was described. Wesley himself stated, "Such a society is no other than a company of men having the form and seeking the power of godliness, united in order to pray together, to receive the word of exhortation, and to watch over one another in love, that they may help each other to work out their own salvation."[11]

Three aspects of this definition are worth noting. First, this is similar to the Class Meeting in that it goes beyond exhortation and includes interaction among the attendees. Second, the definition does not mention Holy Communion, and nowhere in the discussion of the Society is it ever mentioned. Wesley did ordain Thomas Coke in order that Methodists in North America might receive the sacrament, but in the British Isles he assumed that others would go to the parish church for this service. Methodist chapels in Great Britain reflected this assumption in that they had a center pulpit—not a divided chancel that included an altar. Third, whereas the Society included all interested persons, over time attendance was limited to serious seekers. Tickets were required and reissued depending on the continued growth in Christian living as determined by one of the Class leaders.

The Class Meeting

By all odds, the Class Meeting was the most influential and distinctive of all Wesley's groups. Originally proposed as a fund-raising scheme in the Bristol Society by Captain Fox, the Class Meeting became a powerful method of cultivating spiritual growth. Leaders were to collect a penny a week from each of the ten or twelve members and supplement the offering of those unable to pay. In addition, they were to assess the progress (or lack of it) in Christian living of each member as they met together. Each member was to seriously attend to every other member's sharing and be willing to offer support and prayer. Membership in Class Meetings was not voluntary—each new Society member was assigned to membership in a Class. In 1742, some time after the adoption of the Class Meeting method to the Foundery Society, Wesley expressed his appreciation in this way: "This was the origin of our classes at London, for which I can never sufficiently praise God, the unspeakable usefulness of the institution having ever since been more and more manifest."[12] Wesley's exuberance has stood the test of time. Many have judged the Class Meeting as the single most powerful and effective idea to have been developed for spiritual growth. In a unique way, it accomplished several goals: pastoral oversight, personal accountability, group support, and idealistic attainment.

Class Meetings took place away from the chapel where the Society gathered. Where possible, membership was geographically organized to facilitate ease of attendance at the weekly meetings. "Meeting the Class" became a priority, and relationships continued for years. The meeting usually began with a short hymn followed by the leader sharing the condition of his or her own spiritual life. Unlike exhortation, as in Society meetings, Class Meetings emphasized personal sharing of each member's ongoing religious experience. What was uniquely true in the eighteenth century is still true wherever Christians meet in Classes. Social class, wealth, ethnicity, age, and gender are ignored. Probably, no other opportunity for such relationships routinely existed in eighteenth century Great Britain or even now.

The Band

The Band used an *affective* mode of interaction. Whereas, the Society focused on instruction and the Class Meeting focused on behavior, the Band focused on feelings and intentions. Unlike the Society, which included everyone, or the Class Meeting, which was organized geographically, the Band was a homogenous small group that included only men or women, married or unmarried, young or old. Participation was voluntary, not obligatory. Persons who were seriously committed Christians who desired to grow in holiness of thought and emotion became members of these Bands. "It could be said metaphorically that the society aimed for the head, the class meeting for the hands, and the band for the heart."[13]

There is a sense in which the Band was most like the Holy Club of Oxford. It was the original group that Wesley had in mind. The environment was one of openness, honesty, self-examination, sharing, and support. Members sought to reflect on their motives, their reactions, their musings, and their true intentions. They were dedicated to bringing their total selves under the will of God, and they were committed to growth in becoming more like Christ. Wesley called it "close conversation."

The Band is the vehicle that most clearly expresses Wesley's goal of spreading "scriptural holiness through the land." The key word here is *holiness*. Wesley was convinced that holiness was the central doctrine that characterized the uniqueness of Methodism. In Wesley's conviction it was possible to attain total perfection of outward morality and inner intention. He labeled this "perfect love."[14]

In contrast with Luther and Calvin, Wesley believed perfection is possible in this life. Luther believed Christians remain sinners until they die, and Calvin believed perfection is possible only in heaven. Wesley was convinced that the grace of God was an active force that could accomplish the intent of God in believers through sanctification here on earth. The Band was the means toward that end.

As stated before, while Wesley remained firm in his conviction that perfection was possible, he was cautious in ever recognizing that anyone had attained that state.

Unfortunately, while the Bands flourished during Wesley's lifetime, they never gained more than limited popularity. Wesley never ceased to promote them in his preaching and among his preachers, but they never attained the popularity of the Class Meetings. Some have suggested that the Band provided the model for group therapy and other self-help groups.

The Select Society

The Select Society was the group of committed Christians Wesley chose to become the standard-bearers for the Methodist movement. They were those leaders of Class Meetings and Bands who were recognized by Wesley as willing and able to delve deeper into the tenets of the faith. Most importantly, Wesley felt the need to have a group where he could share his own struggles and his concerns. He selected a group of persons to meet with him every Monday morning for an hour. Unlike the Class Meetings and the Bands, there were no procedural rules for this Select Society. It did not even have a leader, although Wesley himself served this role in point of fact. In Select Societies there were three basic assumptions: (1) what was discussed in the meetings was to be held in strictest confidence, (2) in all discussion of inconsequential matters, members agreed to abide by the opinion of the senior minister, and (3) everyone agreed to contribute to the discussions.

Henderson (1997) commented extensively on the function of the Select Society in Wesley's personal understanding of leadership. Wesley did not want to be adored or adulated by his followers. He was wary of becoming a leader whom persons were afraid to be frank with. He wanted open evaluation of how he was being perceived and how the Societies were functioning. He invited help in his own quest for holiness. He sought advice about strategy as the movement grew. Wesley wrote sparingly about the Select Society in his journal, and there were no stated rules for reports of its functioning—as might be expected in a group where confidence was the rule.

Interestingly, there seems to have been Select Societies in many locations. Membership was very heterogeneous and included both men and women. A Negro woman in the Whitehaven Select Society was noted by Wesley as having been especially helpful to him.[15] How Wesley was able to continue meeting with so many Select Societies is unclear. This type of group disappeared with Wesley's death.

The Penitent Band

Wesley intuitively realized that abiding by the challenges of the Class Meetings would prove difficult for some (if not many). He realized there would be those who returned to sinful ways. Others would feel caught in compulsive habits that were difficult to break. Gaining the willpower to change lifestyles was not easy for a number of persons who responded appreciatively to Wesley's preaching. For these persons Wesley established an entirely different kind of group. He called it the *Penitent Band*, which would meet every Saturday night—the night of greatest temptation for many of them.

Those who met in the Penitent Bands agreed to submit entirely to the assessment and recommendations of the senior minister. The minister would determine what was needed to deal with the moral problems of the members. These meetings were very formal, and the hymns, prayers, and teachings were designed to apply to the types of problems the members were experiencing. The functioning of the Penitent Bands probably resembled today's Alcoholics Anonymous. There are few records of these groups, although they seem to have continued for a number of years in certain areas.

Conclusion

This model of Wesley's organizing genius is probably his most enduring contribution to church life. His insight into the manner in which personality is formed and character is changed marks him as a skilled social psychologist—long before there was such a title. The Class Meeting continued to epitomize Methodism well into the nineteenth century, but the other groups passed away fairly quickly after Wesley's death. Nevertheless, again and again there have been many attempts to establish groups similar to each of those in his model—with varying degrees of success. Few would quarrel, however, with Whitefield's judgment that the groups established by Wesley were the key to the success of the Methodist movement, while the results of his (Whitefield's) evangelism faded away. It is noteworthy in evaluating this facet of Wesley's life to realize that he began to face many of the limitations of group life that we face today—namely, time for attending meetings, differences in member needs, geographic limitations, and many demands on leaders' time.

Of course, this survey of Wesley's organizing skills focuses largely on members. His organization of the movement itself also shows how intentional he was in his approach. To avoid members becoming involved with debt, Wesley quickly changed the deeds from groups of trustees to himself as the sole trustee. All chapels included a deed declaration to Wesley, who, in turn, transferred the legal ownership to a select body of preachers called the *Legal Hundred*. This practice is continued today in that church property belongs to the denomination. Although Wesley did not mention it, this practice is a form of ensuring that the property will be used in accord with Methodism.

Yet another facet of Wesley's organizing method can be seen in the way he organized the movement itself as growth occurred. In 1744 he and his brother Charles called together four clergy and four lay preachers for a consultation. This was the first of the annual conferences that characterize Methodism. Only two years later, Wesley initiated the appointment system that is still in vogue. Called the *itinerancy,* Wesley divided the Societies into groups and assigned helpers who would make at least thirty contacts a month. Since he believed that Societies would benefit from a variety of leaders, he decided that these helpers would stay for a period of two years and then be reassigned to another group. This practice is still the Methodist model, although many ministers stay for longer periods.

4
John Wesley the Physician[1]

Although his professional identity was not that of a physician, out of a persistent concern for the plight of the poor, Wesley became a leader in promoting both emotional and physical health in Great Britain. He wrote a volume entitled *Primitive Physick: Or an Easy and Natural Method of Curing Most Diseases* (1747). In this book he advocated a number of surprisingly modern practices for healthy living and sickness prevention along with recommending a variety of simple cures for over 250 illnesses. In the eighteenth and early nineteenth centuries Wesley's book sold more than any other medical handbook and could be found in almost all British homes, particularly those of the poor.

Many of his admonitions could be placed in current textbooks of health psychology with little or no adaptation. Wesley dealt with every major area in the field as defined by Matarazzo (1982).[2] This definition given below provides a set of topics under which Wesley's contributions can be considered. These are (1) the promotion and maintenance of health, (2) the prevention and treatment of illness, (3) the identification of etiologic and diagnostic correlates of health, illness, and related dysfunction, and (4) the analysis and improvement of the health-care system and health policy formation. Before we consider Wesley's ideas and writings on each of these topics, some aspects of his background are appropriate to detail.

John Wesley's Interest in Health

The Great Britain of Wesley's time was a field ripe for concern about both social justice and human welfare. Wilder (1978) described some of these conditions.

> It was an age of immorality for England. . . . Sir William Blackstone, the great jurist, went to hear every clergyman of note in London out of curiosity and "did not hear a single discourse which had more Christianity in it than the writings of Cicero;" and it would have been impossible for him to discover from what he heard "whether the preacher were a follower of Confucius, or Mohammed, or of Christ." . . . The court circles were characterized by open bribery and corruption. . . . Adultery was the rule rather than the exception among the ruling and wealthy classes. Drunkenness was looked upon with every tolerance, almost with admiration. It was even worse with the poorer classes. Every sixth house in London was a gin shop. . . . Human life was cheap; law was severe. Over two hundred crimes, including petty theft, called for the death penalty. . . . Women, for some crimes, were "publicly burned." The slave trade, brutal and horrible, reached its zenith during this period. Over four thousand men were imprisoned each year.[3]

In eighteenth-century England, public hygiene was abominable. Open sewage and excrement from horses cluttered many streets. Sanitary conditions for personal toileting were very primitive. Food was often contaminated. Diet was poor and contained a lot of fat. Epidemics were common, and medical treatment was expensive and rare. There was great disparity among the social classes. The Industrial Revolution was surging, and working conditions were harsh. Child labor was rampant. Hopelessness among the common people was the order of the day. In fact, depression was widespread.

It is noteworthy that although Wesley was privileged, in the sense that he was able to enjoy an Oxford education, his personal desire to be a holy person, coupled with his concern to preach to the masses after his May 24, 1738, religious experience, propelled him into compulsive action in behalf of the physical, as well as the spiritual and emotional, health of the average citizen. Wesley "forsook the seclusion of Oxford Halls to bear to the miners and fishermen, to the common people in general, a new religious life."[4]

And this new religious life included a life free from physical illness—a life lived in conditions of cleanliness, justice, and emotional well-being. Wesley is credited with originating the saying "Cleanliness is next to godliness." In an essay on the nineteenth-century crusade against dirt, a professor of preventive medicine noted that a hundred years before, John Wesley had "fought his great fight for hygiene—he was the greatest health educator of the eighteenth century in Britain."[5] Vanderpool (1986) concurred with this assessment: "More than any other major figure in Christendom, John Wesley actively involved himself with the theory and practice of medicine as well as the principles and practice of ideal physical and mental health."[6]

A widespread health movement followed his work,[7] and many historians would agree with the statement that in matters of "hygiene and preventive medicine Wesley is an acknowledged pioneer, a voice crying in the wilderness . . . a voice of great power and penetration because of the enormous personal influence he came to have throughout the whole nation."[8] As an indication of his popularity, Wesley's book, *Primitive Physick* (1747) went through thirty-eight English and twenty-four American editions before it took its place as a quaint artifact on library back shelves in the mid-nineteenth century.

As a clergyperson, Wesley's involvement in medical matters might seem disturbing and inappropriate were it not for the fact that it was common in the seventeenth and eighteenth centuries for village parsons and lords-of-the-manor to act as healers for those under their care, who were poor or far removed from physicians' offices.[9] Moreover, Wesley was widely read in medical matters. He had always had a secret desire to be a doctor and had begun serious reading of medical texts in his spare time soon after entering Oxford as a student. The preface to his *Primitive Physick* is a thorough summary of the history of medicine and the cures he recommended, which are quaint in light of modern procedures but are a respectable reflection of medical treatment in his day.[10]

Wesley contended that most physicians were interested only in making money. He was convinced that they collaborated with the apothecaries in prescribing complicated drugs that often did little good. Wesley wrote two letters defending his practice of "physic" (i.e., healing) that negatively depict physicians. His statements include the following:

> Neither Jesus nor His disciples derived their authority
> from the national licensing corporation of their day.
> . . . Licensing bodies may be set up as social safeguards
> or as protection for private interests. . . . Unrecognized
> authority may by-pass them or sweep them aside. . . .
> For more than twenty years I had numberless proofs

that regular physicians do exceedingly little good. From a deep conviction of this I have believed it my duty within these four months last past to prescribe such medicines to 600–700 of the poor as I knew were proper for their several disorders. Within six weeks nine in ten of them who had taken these medicines were remarkably altered for the better and many were cured of diseases under which they had labored 10, 20, 40 years. Now, ought I have let one of these poor wretches perish because I was not a regular physician? To have said, 'I know what will cure you, but I am not of the College; You must send for Doctor Mead'? Before Dr. Mead had come in his chariot the man might have been in his coffin.[11]

Wesley's Ideas about the Promotion and Maintenance of Health

Very early in his student days at Oxford, Wesley came under the influence of George Cheyne's book *An Essay on Health and Long Life* (1724). Cheyne (1671–1743) was a well-known Bath physician whose popular medical writings "preached temperance to an intemperate generation."[12] Cheyne was a convert to his own teachings. After giving up preparing for the ministry and becoming a physician, Cheyne had set up practice in London, where his habits exemplified Wesley's negative judgments about selfishness and greed. He eventually weighed over 350 pounds because of heavy drinking and rich eating. Even after strict abstention and "a course of waters at Bath," he slipped back into such obesity that he could hardly breathe and could scarcely walk. He recovered by dieting on milk and vegetables. This led him to write his book, which was the first medical book written for popular consumption in England.

Wesley arranged his own life in accordance with Cheyne's prescriptions. He wrote his mother about his enthusiasm: "I suppose you have seen the famous Dr. Cheyne's book of *Health and Long Life*. . . . He refers almost everything to temperance and exercise and supports most things with physical reasons. . . . He entirely condemns eating anything salty or highly seasoned, as also pork, fish, and stall-fed cattle and also recommends for drink two pints of water and one of wine in twenty-four hours . . . in consequence of Dr. Cheyne I chose to eat sparingly and to drink water."[13]

Cheyne recommended six habits: breathe pure air, eat and drink temperately, sleep plentifully, exercise abundantly, evacuate and excrete without obstruction, and control the expression of the passions (i.e., emotions).[14] Wesley practiced these faithfully. He exercised daily, often went for a swim in the river, drank much water, and ate little. He even later advised the preachers in his movement to retire early and to "kill themselves a little each day" by eating less than they wanted.

Wesley devoted a chapter to each of Cheyne's six health habits in his *Primitive Physick*. These habits were known as the "nonnaturals" for two reasons.[15] In the first place, they are unnatural in the sense that they confront the natural inclination to gorge and be intemperate in self-expression. Wesley even commented that people would likely pay little attention to Cheyne's book because it advised against eating and drinking. In the second place, they are unnatural, according to Wesley, because they are the laws of health given by God. It is God's intention that humans fulfill their created potentials through long and healthy lives. Along with Plato, Wesley felt that health is a secondary, not a primary, virtue. Health is the means by which humans are able to do what God intends them to do and to be, but not an end in itself.

Wesley understood the importance of the human body from the biblical statement that the body is the temple of the Holy

Spirit (1 Corinthians 6:19), meaning that people's bodies are to be treated with great respect because they are the sacred buildings in which the Spirit of God resides. Although perfect health was the state Adam and Eve enjoyed in the garden of Eden, the fall brought illness. Therefore a sensible regimen, based on the discipline of the non-naturals, was the God-appointed pattern for healthy living, according to Wesley.

Wesley attributed most sickness to a violation of these six non-naturals. He came close to equating lack of care of the body with sin. The name *Methodist*, a label of derision ascribed to him and his followers, was due, in no small measure, to the exactness in manner of living, that is, the *method*, he recommended. Wesley himself perceived the name as quite appropriate since the label could be said to refer to an ancient sect of physicians called Methodists, who believed that most diseases could be cured by exercise and diet. Many would agree with the assessment that these rules for preventing illness and sustaining health "would serve as admirably now as then."[16]

Wesley's Ideas about the Prevention and Treatment of Illness

These comments about Wesley's concern for self-control, diet, and exercise lead naturally into a discussion of the second of Matarazzo's topics in his definition of health psychology, namely, the issues of prevention and treatment. Since prevention was related in the previous section to adherence to the non-naturals and will be considered in the section on the health-care system, the present discussion will deal largely with treatment.

As noted earlier, Wesley was no stranger to medical matters. His interest changed from curiosity to a central focus when he began preparing for a missionary assignment in Georgia in the early

1730s. He had hopes of being "some service to those who had no regular physician among them."[17] While in Georgia he participated in, at least, one autopsy and studied the healing practices of the Indians. He was convinced that native peoples were uncontaminated by the "theoretical medicine" of such cultures as England and that they used simple, effective methods of healing that could be applied by anyone willing to use them. Vanderpool (1986) noted that Wesley asserted, "'Ancient or primitive medical remedies have certain basic characteristics. . . . They are efficacious and useful because they are founded upon trial-and-error experiments and experience. They are plain, simple, safe, and inexpensive, because they are readily found in ordinary plants, animals, and inorganic substances.' These qualities paralleled the 'plain and simple' Gospel proclaimed by Wesley, a Gospel unfettered by theological abstractions, available to all humans irrespective of wealth or station in life, curative for body and soul."[18]

This search for proven methods of healing became the guiding principle in his book *Primitive Physick*. The title of this book portrays its content. *Physick* is a synonym for healing, and *Primitive* refers to its origins in those ancient methods handed down from father to son. Wesley felt that cures based on these methods were better for two reasons. First, they utilized procedures and materials that were accessible and available in the natural world. Second, they had been pragmatically tried and demonstrated to be valid in treating disease.

Wesley's chief complaint about physicians of his day was that they depended on theory rather than proof for their treatments. He perceived, somewhat correctly, that eighteenth-century medicine was still preoccupied with a humoral theory of disease, which concluded that illness was due to an imbalance of body humors. Humoral balance, in turn, could be restored by ingestion of the many chemicals that were being concocted and stored at the apothecaries. Although greatly concerned with these theories of disease and treatment, medicine at this time was not as unpragmatic as Wesley contended. Physicians were functionally oriented and did continue to prescribe new drugs when the old ones didn't work. Wesley's contention was that this process led to great expense and danger for the patient. Wesley's recommendation was that physicians needed to use the proven methods of folk medicine. Not only were these approaches cheaper, but they had already gone through generations of trial and error.

It is noteworthy that this approach by Wesley was almost atheoretical in its pragmatism. He was not concerned with why a healing method worked—only that it did. Some labeled him "empiric"; he called himself "experimental." In our contemporary understanding of these terms, *empiric* is probably far more correct than *experimental*. In no way could Wesley be called experimental if that term means an approach whereby conditions are controlled and the tenets of a theory are tested. At best, Wesley was a trial-and-error pragmatist, not an experimentalist.

Nevertheless, he recommended an approach that, in some ways, was very enlightened in that he provided in his book several cures for each of the 288 illnesses he described. He based these lists of possible treatments on the premise that not every cure works for every person. Nor do some cures work on every occasion. Wesley suggested that the ill person should try one of the recommendations and if that did not work try another. In a somewhat curious manner, he marked some of the nine hundred treatments with the letter *T* (Tried) and some with *I* (Infallible), as if some of the unmarked treatments had not been subjected to experiment or as if some other treatments had been tried but worked only part of the time. These markings might seem a violation of his methodology and a humble admission that only a very few treatments work every time.

Turning to the recommended treatments themselves, judgments about their validity were, and are, mixed. It should come as no surprise that Wesley's negative criticism of physicians should be matched, among physicians, by equally negative reactions to his medical dabbling. Hill (1958) quoted the evaluation of one author who judged Wesley and his followers to be naive, anti-intellectual, and dangerous to society. *Primitive Physick* was pictured as "a little book, on sale at all Methodist meeting houses; an absurd, fantastic compilation of uncritical folklore."[19]

One humorous interaction occurred in the mid-1770s. William Hawes, a well-known physician to the London Dispensary, accused Wesley of being a quack and published a disparaging review of Wesley's book in a 1776 issue of *Lloyd's Evening Post*. Wesley replied by letter: "Dear Sir, My bookseller informs me that since you published your remarks on the *Primitive Physick*, there has been a greater demand than ever. If, therefore, you please to publish a few further remarks you would confer a favor upon your Humble Servant."[20] The public's reaction to Hawes's criticism implies that Wesley was not the only one who distrusted the opinions of medical professionals.

Two evaluations in the early years of the twentieth century illustrate that some in the medical profession still retained a disdain for Wesley's ideas, and others had come to see his treatment recommendations in less negative ways. Thomas (1906), writing in the *American Physician*, concluded that "there was something undignified in this preoccupation with bodily ailments and this meddling with their cure on the part of one capable of exercising so profound an influence on his generation as Wesley." He further offered, "There is nothing in the book of any value whatsoever, and, curiously nothing that might not have been written by a person with the slightest education and meanest intellect."[21] Yet Riddell (1914), writing in the *New York Medical Journal* only a few years later, reached a decidedly different conclusion. He stated, "It will be found that Wesley's treatment of diseases was at least as reconcilable with common sense as that of the contemporary regular practitioner, much more so in some cases. Of it, at least, it could be said . . . 'It did no great harm.'"[22]

Riddell noted that although Wesley was generally critical of physicians, Riddell, nevertheless, contended that Wesley's prescriptions were intended for those with chronic illnesses that had not been alleviated and that in the case of acute or life-threatening sickness a person should seek the services of a "doctor who fears God."

So it can be said that while a number of Wesley's treatments did indeed rely on folklore, many of his treatments were in accord with the medicine of his day. Although they may seem quaint to us, they do not appear so when compared with much that was current in the 1700s. Rousseau compared Wesley's recommendations to the writings of six medical authorities of the same century and stated, "When discussed in this context, Wesley's treatise does not suffer."[23] Of note is the fact that he disparaged some of the more radical treatments used by his contemporaries such as bloodletting and quicksilver.

Three examples of Wesley's prescriptions from *Primitive Physick* will serve to illustrate his approach. The 288 illnesses are arranged in alphabetical order like a dictionary. There are as few as one and as many as ten prescriptions provided for each of the maladies.

A Chronical Head-ach

Keep your Feet in *warm Water*, a Quarter of Hour before you go to Bed; for two or three Weeks; or wear tender *Hemlock-leaves*, under the Feet changing them daily; or order a Tea-kettle of *cold Water* to be pour'd on your Head every Morning in a slender stream; or apply to the Head bruised *Cummin-seed*, fried with an Egg; or take a large Tea-cup full of *Carduus* Tea without Sugar fasting for six or seven mornings; or boil *Wood-betony* in new Milk and strain it. Breakfast on this for five or six Weeks.[24]

Small Pox

Drink largely of Toast and Water; or Let your constant drink be milk and water mixt; or The best food is Milk and Apples; or Bread dipped in Milk and water; Take care to have a free, pure, and cool Air. Therefore open the casement every day, only do not let it chill the patient. If they strike in, and convulsions follows, drink a pint of cold water immediately. This instantly stops the convulsions, and drives out the pock. Lentils and Rape-weeds are a certain cure for small pox.[25]

A Stubborn Ulcer

Burn to ashes (but not too long) the gross stalks on which the *red Coleworts* grow. Make a Plaister with this and fresh Butter. Change it once a Day. Or apply a Poultis of boil'd *Parsnips*. This will cure even when the Bone is foul. [26]

Primitive Physick is replete with remedies that would still be in vogue today. These include cold-water bathing, poultices, hot and cold drinks, purges, and drugs made from ingredients found in most kitchens. Of course, there are other remedies, such as cow dung, ground-up spiderwebs, and crushed-up warts found on the inside of horses legs, that appear curious and unusual.

The lists include amusing treatments such as those recommended for consumption and head cold. For the former Wesley recommended, "Every morning cut a little turf of fresh earth, and, laying down, breathe in the hole for a quarter of an hour."[27] For the latter Wesley recommended, "Pare very thin the yellow rind of an orange, roll it up inside out and thrust a roll into each nostril."[28] An enticing recommendation for stomachache was to lie with a live puppy resting on the stomach. He even included several treatments for aging that ended with "death—which is the final cure."

Of immense interest to modern health psychology are Wesley's prescriptions for nervous disorders. Here Wesley asserted that nervous disorders "are of two kinds: 1. Those which proceed from the Nerves being compressed by the swelling of the muscular flesh; Or, 2. When the Nerves themselves are disordered. In the former case, Temperance and Abstemiousness will generally cure; In the latter, when the Nerves perform their office too languidly, a GOOD AIR is the first requisite. The patients also should rise early, and as soon as the Dew is off the ground, walk."

Wesley followed these admonitions with several paragraphs concerning diet and tincture made from valerian root and powder from mistletoe. He concluded with the following statement: "But I am firmly persuaded, there is no remedy in Nature, for Nervous Disorders of every kind, comparable to the proper and constant use of the Electrical Machine."[29]

This unexpected recommendation for shocking sick persons is likely the least well-known and most controversial of Wesley's remedies. On the surface, it would seem as if Wesley was anticipating the use of electroconvulsive shock treatment in psychiatry by over a hundred years. This is only partly true. More correct is the judgment by Hill that Wesley was one of the most outstanding general electrotherapists of the eighteenth century.[30] He did embrace the general use of static electric shock when only a very few physicians had done so but cautioned against the overly strong shocks that have come to characterize ECT today.

Wesley's Ideas about the Etiology and Diagnosis of Health and Illness

The third aspect of Matarazzo's definition of health psychology pertains to the etiologic and diagnostic correlates of health and illness. Here, too, John Wesley had much to say that is relevant to the history of the field. On the one hand, he had an awareness of what would be termed today psychosomatics. On the other hand, he had a deep appreciation for the part that the physical environment plays in both helping persons recover from illness and preventing their becoming sick again.

Wesley's awareness of psychosomatics is nowhere better exemplified than in a case study in his journal reported by Hill:

> Reflecting today on the case of a poor woman who had continual pain in her stomach. I could not but remark on the inexcusable negligence of most physicians in cases of this nature. They prescribe drug after drug, without knowing a jot of the matter about the root of the disorder, and without knowing this they cannot cure, though they can murder the patient. Whence came this woman's pain (which she would never have told had she been questioned about it)? From fretting for the death of her son. And what availed medicines while that fretting continued? Why then do not all physicians consider how far bodily disorders are caused or influenced by the mind, and in those cases which are utterly out of their sphere call in the assistance of the ministers; as ministers, when they find the mind disordered by the body, call in the assistance of the physicians?[31]

Toward the close of the preface to his book *Primitive Physick*, Wesley summed up his ideas regarding the relationship between the mind and the body, between the emotions—called passions—and health. He stated: "1. The Passions have a greater Influence on Health than most People are aware of. 2. All violent and sudden Passions dispose to, or actually throw People into Acute Diseases. 3. The slow and lasting Passions, such as Grief and hopeless Love, bring on Chronic Diseases. 4. Till the Passion which caused the Disease is calmed, medicine is applied in vain."[32]

Wesley seems to have adopted a theory of maintenance and moderation. Ideally persons who experience strong emotions of any kind should do so infrequently and only for short periods of time if they would maintain their health. Sustained strong emotions work havoc on the body. Wesley offered no theory of how this happens, but he definitely anticipated what is known today about stress reactions and the response of the parasympathetic nervous system to threat.

Subsequent to these comments on the emotions, Wesley added a comment about the emotion, or passion, par excellence, namely, "the love of God." Here he was writing not about an emotion humans have toward God, but an emotion God has toward persons—to which humans can respond. He called God's love the "Sovereign Remedy of all Miseries." His rationale is as follows: "Or in particular it [the love of God] effectually prevents all the Bodily Disorders the Passions introduce, by keeping the Passions themselves within due Bounds. And by unspeakable Joy and perfect Calm, Serenity and Tranquility it gives the mind, it becomes the most powerful of all the Means of Health and Long Life."[33]

While Wesley's Christian presuppositions about the nature of the divine would by no means be shared by all contemporary health psychologists, the value of a philosophy of life that avails persons of inner strength over and beyond the exigencies of experience is a valid component of modern stress management and problem-solving programs. Wesley, quite correctly, perceived that experiencing reassuring affirmation from a source beyond environmental stressors works toward "keeping the Passions themselves within due Bounds" and provides "Calm, Serenity and Tranquility." The process he described has been validated by modern approaches to the reduction of stress.

In addition to these ideas about psychosomatic relationships, Wesley had strong ideas about how the environment handicapped or enhanced treatment. He not only despaired about the unavailability of physicians for those who could not pay, but also recognized that hospitals were often places where people became sicker rather than better. It was very common for hospitalized patients to contract "hospital fever," a lethal form of typhus. Conditions were appalling. Sanitary conditions were crude. Smells were offensive. Nurses were ignorant about the spread of infection.

Taking his cues from the writing of Simone-Andre Tissot, a Swiss physician, on prevention and cure, Wesley detailed a set of conditions that would speed treatment and avoid complications. These recommendations included cautions about overheating the room and keeping patients in closed rooms where the air would become foul "whereby so many diseases are heightened and prolonged and so many thousands of lives thrown away."[34] He surmised that bad nursing often impeded healing. He was against forcing patients to eat, inducing vomiting, and sweating. He advocated fresh air, water, and leaving the stomach alone so it would not become inflamed. He recommended plenty to drink, light food, and sleeping on a pallet—no feathers—and covered only with sheets. He advised making the bed daily, changing the sheets every other day, and eating a variety of fruits during the feverish stages. He cautioned against breathing near the face of those who were sick. By these simple methods he concluded that many acute diseases could be mitigated, if not cured.

Wesley even had advice for the regimen to follow in case of major illnesses such as pneumonia. In addition to seeking a "physician who fears God," he recommended "drinking lukewarm barley water often, taking 10 ounces of oxymel of squills added to 50 ounces of elder flowers in fusion every two hours and applying a poultice of boiled bread, milk and hot water to the breast and throat. In extreme sickness he advised taking a spoonful of a mixture of 60 ounces of syrup of violets and 10 ounces of spirit of sulfur in barley water."[35]

In regard to the living conditions that might cause illness, Wesley showed that he had done a thorough survey of typical working and living conditions. He advised against persisting too long at fatiguing labor, resting in a cold place after becoming overheated, drinking cold water when one was very hot, and getting drunk or being intemperate in eating. He noted that changes in the weather, failing to air lodgings, having ditches too close to the window, eating bad grain or badly cooked bread, and constructing a house too close to the ground were all dangers to be avoided.

Wesley propagated these ideas in numerous pamphlets and in teachings at meetings of the Methodist Societies to which many people came. Hill concluded that because of Wesley's influence, "thousands were so changed that, along with a spiritual renaissance, there was a desire for higher mental and physical standards."[36] The leaders of the Societies were encouraged to be models of good health practices. Wesley quaintly advised one leader in Northern Ireland,

> If you regard your health, touch no supper but a little milk or water gruel. This will by the blessing of God secure you from nervous disorders. . . . Avoid all familiarity with women. This is deadly poison both to them and you. You cannot be too wary in this respect. . . . Avoid all nastiness, dirt, slovenliness. . . . Do not

stink above ground. . . . Whatever clothes you have,
let them be whole. . . . Let none ever see a ragged
Methodist. Clean yourself of lice. . . . Do not cut off
your hair, but clean it, and keep it clean. Cure yourself
and your family of the itch: a spoonful of brimstone
will cure you. . . . Use no tobacco unless prescribed
by a physician. It is an uncleanly and unwholesome
self-indulgence. . . . Use no snuff. . . . Touch no dram.
It is liquid fire . . . a sure though slow poison.[37]

Wesley's Analysis and Improvement
of the Health-Care System

Wesley was an extremely socially sensitive person. Almost all aspects
of life in eighteenth-century England came under his scrutiny.
Soon after his religious experience in 1738, he returned to Oxford
and preached sermons that were sharply critical of the university's
lack of concern for the plight of the average person.

Wherever Wesley went, he made statements about social
injustice. At Stoke-on-Trent he spoke out against working conditions and corruption in the pottery industry there. At Penzance he
confronted citizens who moved lighthouses and then plundered
the shipwrecks. He addressed the slave trade and deplorable prison
conditions and established a savings society that gave interest-free
loans to the poor. So, it should come as no surprise that his protests
should extend to the health-care system.

He was very critical of physicians and druggists. After tracing
the corruption of simple remedies by medical theories, he stated in
the preface to *Primitive Physick*:

Is it inquired, But are there not Books enough already,
on every Part of the Art of Medicine? Yes, too many,
ten Times over, considering how little to the Purpose

the far greater Part of them speak. But beside this,
they are so dear (expensive) for the poor Men to buy,
and too hard for plain Men to understand. . . . In all
[the books] that have yet fallen into my Hands, I find
many dear and many farfetched Medicines; many of
so dangerous a Kind, as a Prudent Man would never
meddle with. And against the greater Part of those
Medicines; there is a further Objection, They consist
of too many Ingredients. This Common Method of
compounding and decompounding Medicines, can
never be reconciled to Common Sense. Experience
shows, That One Thing will cure most Disorders,
at least as well as Twenty put together. Then why
do you add the other Nineteen? only to swell the
Apothecary Bill: Nay, possibly, on Purpose to prolong
the Distemper, that the Doctor and he may divide
the Spoil.[38]

To meet this need for cheaper and more available health care,
Wesley wrote his book. He called himself both "God's steward for
the poor" and "a lover of mankind." A more admirable motive
for improving the social system would be hard to find. He went
a step beyond writing about treatment and prevention, however.
He made attending to the sick a central focus of the groups that
he organized.

One of the chief duties of the leaders of Methodist Societies
was to visit the sick. Wesley found, however, that this task for the
stewards to attend to all who were sick was too big in addition to
their other obligations. So he divided London into twenty-three
districts and commissioned sixty-four leaders whom he "judged
to be of the most tender, loving spirit" to be official visitors of the
sick. In his usual compulsive manner, Wesley mandated that each

visitor would see the sick in his or her district three times a week. Their task was to "inquire into their disorders, and procure advice for them, and to do anything for them which might add to their comfort."[39] This plan was Wesley's own health-care system.

The system was only partially successful. It was more palliative than ameliorative. Wesley wrote, "I was still in pain for many of the poor that were sick; there was so great expense. And, first, I resolved to try whether they might not receive more benefit in the hospitals. Upon the trial, we found there was indeed less expense, but no more good done than before. I then asked the advice of several Physicians for them. But still it profited not. I saw the poor people pining away, and several families ruined, and that without remedy."[40]

In response to his own troubled reflections on the lack of treatment for the poor, Wesley set up free clinics in Bristol and London. His first dispensary for the poor was actually established in 1746, one year before the publication of *Primitive Physick*. He recorded his deliberations: "At length I thought of a kind of desperate expedient: 'I will prepare and give them physic myself . . . and took unto my assistance an Apothecary, and an experienced Surgeon; resolving, at the same time, not to go out of my depth, but to leave all difficult and complicated cases to such medical attendants as the patient should choose."[41]

Dunlop described the first day the clinic opened in this account:

> Thirty patients were waiting when the doors first opened. William Kirman, an aged weaver, who lived on Old Nichol Street, shuffled up to be treated.
>
> "What complaint have you?" asked Wesley.
>
> "Oh, sir, a cough, a very sore cough. I can get no rest night or day."
>
> "How long have you had it?"

"About three-score years; it began when I was 11 years old."

Wesley gave the old weaver a harmless drug. His first patient was not likely to be a problem. "Take this three or four times a day. If it does you no good, it will do you no harm," he said.

The old man took the drug and later reported to Wesley that he had been cured.[42]

During the first month over three hundred patients came. Over five hundred came during the first six months. Expenses for medications were about forty pounds. Eventually, Wesley established four clinics in London and one in Bristol. It is noteworthy that Wesley earned over 150,000 pounds from his writings but spent almost all of it on human welfare projects. He died with little money left.

Although the clinics did not survive his death, this effort to improve health-care delivery is significant testimony to his responsible involvement in human welfare.

Conclusion

One writer summed up Wesley's contribution by stating, "He found the great masses without help in time of distress, and failing a more satisfactory solution, he set himself with characteristic energy and thoroughness to the task. He did much to direct the attention of the public to the importance of health and he pointed to the source from which help must come. As a layman, he has earned, I think, an honored place in the history of medicine."[43] And we might add that Wesley has earned an honored place in the history of health psychology, as well.

5

John Wesley the Electrotherapist[1]

John Wesley pioneered the use of electric shock for the treatment of illness. In 1760 he published *The Desideratum: Or Electricity Made Plain and Useful by a Lover of Mankind and of Common Sense* based on his use of electricity in free medical clinics he had established for the poor in Bristol and London a decade earlier. Having become excited by the therapeutic potential of Benjamin Franklin's demonstrations, Wesley reported in his diary of November 9, 1756, that he obtained a portable electrical apparatus "on purpose." Out of a conviction that he had discovered a cheap and easy way to treat many diseases, he wrote:

> I ordered several persons to be electrified, who were ill of various disorders; some of whom found an immediate, some a gradual cure. From this time I appointed, first some hours in every week, and afterward an hour in every day, wherein any that desired it might try the virtue of this surprising medicine. Two or three years

after, our patients were so numerous that we were obliged to divide them; so part were electrified in Southwark, part at the Foundery, others near St. Paul, and the rest near the Seven Dials. The same method we have taken ever since; and to this day, while hundreds, perhaps thousands, have received unspeakable good, I have not known one man, woman, or child, who has received hurt thereby.[2]

Several authors (Hill, 1958; Schiller, 1981;[3] Tyerman, 1870) credit Wesley with playing a previously unacknowledged role in medical and psychiatric history and with being among the greatest electrotherapists of the 1700s. Hunter (1957) noted that seven years after the publication of Wesley's *Desideratum* Middlesex Hospital in London had purchased an electrical machine for use in the training of physicians. Hunter reported that "by the later 1780s electrotherapy had . . . become the stock in trade of many physicians . . . [and] by 1793 the citizens of London had subscribed toward the foundation of The London Electrical Dispensary . . . with a view to afford a new benefit to the lower orders of mankind. . . . It is to administer electricity for all complaints in which its application may be useful."[4]

Over three thousand patients were treated in this dispensary during the following decade. In the preface to his book, Wesley stated that he was aware that electricity would not cure all disorders. "Indeed," he wrote, "there cannot be in Nature any such Thing as an absolute Panacea. . . . I doubt not, but more nervous Disorders would be cured in one Year, by this single Remedy, than the whole English Materia Medica will cure, by the End of the century."[5]

This chapter discusses Wesley's electrotherapeutic activity as a unique episode in the historical development of therapeutic theory. Although Wesley suggested in his book *Primitive Physick: Or an Easy and Natural Method of Curing Most Diseases* (1747) that electric shock was beneficial to over twenty maladies, he felt it was particularly effective in the treatment of nervous disorders. Of particular interest in this discussion will be the question of whether Wesley's ideas are related to the development of electroconvulsive shock treatment in psychiatry. Hackman (1978) is convinced that the two are unrelated,[6] and Hunter (1957) boldly asserted that "the spirit of electrical treatment of mental illness today is in direct contrast to Wesley's kindly and humanitarian efforts to bring hope, if not aid, to the sick and suffering with fairly innocuous electric currents and shocks."[7] He further contended that electroconvulsive shock treatment is "a descendent of the crude and violent methods to which the insane were subjected before the great lunacy reforms of the mid-nineteenth century, when they used to be shocked into unconsciousness by excessive bleeding, holding under water, dropping from a height or spinning in a revolving chair, in order as it was hoped to shock them back into their senses."

On the other hand, Stainbrook (1948) took the opposite point of view in contending that Wesley's application of electricity to sickness was a precursor to psychiatry's electroconvulsive shock treatments of the insane.[8]

This discussion will be divided into sections that consider the development of Wesley's interest in electricity, the equipment and method he used, Wesley's reasoning that electricity was the God-given, "vital elixir" of life, his application of electric shock to suffering and illness, and the influence of Wesley on subsequent electrotherapy.

The Development of Wesley's Interest in Electricity

John Wesley had broad interests and was conversant across a number of fields. In his preaching and promotion of Methodist

Societies, he reportedly traveled over fifty thousand miles each year by horseback across England, Scotland, Ireland, and Wales—always reading as he went. When given a carriage, Wesley boarded up one side and made a bookcase out of it so that he could have more access to a variety of books while he traveled.

Wesley was not only versed in classical and contemporary religious literature, but also well acquainted with scientific and medical writings. He was also knowledgeable about natural science. He understood current thinking, and in a five-volume text entitled *A Survey of the Wisdom of God in the Creation: Or a Compendium of Natural Philosophy* (1777), Wesley summarized the theory of "the great Newton." In fact, Wesley was so broad in his interests that some have considered him expansive and a dilettante who was constantly seduced by the "newfangled."

It should come as no surprise, therefore, that Wesley should be among those who were captivated by the public demonstrations of electrical phenomena that were extremely popular in the second quarter of the eighteenth century in England. Frictional electrical machines had been improved to the point where they were portable and available for astonishing the public by igniting ether and brandy via sparks from fingers. Among the more dramatic demonstrations was the simultaneous leaping of a charge across a mile-long group of monks holding an iron wire connected to a Leyden jar that contained frictional electricity. One letter of the time contended that these public spectacles were "the universal topic of discourse. The fine ladies forget their cards and scandal to talk of the effects of electricity."[9]

Wesley became intrigued with these demonstrations. His journal records that in October 1747 he went with friends to see some of these experiments and became deeply impressed. He wrote, "Who can comprehend how fire lives in water and passes through it more freely than through air? How flame issues from my finger, real flame, such as sets fire to spirits of wine? How these, and many more strange phenomena, arise from the turning of a glass globe?"[10]

His interest was piqued by the letters of Benjamin Franklin (1760) to Peter Collison, a member of the British Royal Society of Science. These letters had been published in pamphlet form as early as 1751. Based on his well-known kite experiment and including a series of subsequent investigations, Franklin's reports excited Wesley. His journal entry for February 17, 1753, stated:

From Dr. Franklin's *Letters* I learned (1) that electric fire (ether) is a species of fire, is finer than any yet known; (2) that it is diffused, and in nearly equal proportions, through almost all substances; (3) that, as long as it is thus diffused, it has no discernible effect; (4) that if any quantity of it be collected together, whether by art or nature, it then becomes visible in the form of fire, and inexpressibly powerful; (5) that it is essentially different from the light of the sun, for it pervades a thousand bodies which light cannot penetrate, and yet cannot penetrate glass, which light pervades so freely; (6) that lightning is none other than electric fire, collected by one or more clouds; (7) that all the effects of lightning may be performed by an artificial electric fire; (8) that anything tracts the lightning, just as a needle does the electric fire; (9) that the electric fire, discharged on a rat or a fowl, will kill it instantly, but discharged on one dipped in water, will slide off, and do it no hurt at all. In like manner the lightning which will kill a man in a moment will not hurt him if he be thoroughly wet. What an amazing scene is here opened for after-ages to improve upon.[11]

Soon after reading Franklin's letters, Wesley himself became part of that after-age improvement. He procured an electrical machine and began to think about its practical application to the alleviation of human suffering. He experimented with the machine by shocking himself for lameness and neuralgia. Cure was certain, but gradual. He advised a person with a "stubborn paralytic disorder" to try the "new remedy." Immediate relief followed. He recorded in his journal, "By the same means I have known two persons cured of an inveterate pain in the stomach, and another of a pain in his side which he had ever since he was a child." Added to this report was another statement of the disdain in which he held the medical practitioners of his day. With these words, Wesley stated that they would probably ignore the value of electricity: "Nevertheless, who can wonder that many gentlemen of the faculty [physicians], as well as their good friends of the apothecaries, decry a medicine so shockingly cheap and easy as much as they do quicksilver and tar-water."[12]

In his desire to provide cheap and easy-to-use remedies for poor people, Wesley provided electric shock machines for all of his free clinics, as noted earlier. On the basis of what he termed "experiment," he noted thirty-seven disorders for which he felt that electricity had been of unquestionable value in curing. Although his claims may seem outlandish to modern ears, he, nevertheless, advised caution in difficult cases and admonished those who administered the shocks to take care not to hurt their patients. In anticipating the later application of electricity to mental illness, Wesley noted that many of those who were helped were of "the nervous kind" and added, "Perhaps there is no nervous distemper whatever which would not yield to a steady use of this remedy."[13]

Wesley's Equipment and Method

Before a discussion of Wesley's theorizing about the nature of electricity and his rationale about its therapeutic effects, it may be helpful to describe the machine and methods that Wesley used. One of these machines is displayed at the museum in the house next to the chapel on City Road, London, where Wesley lived for the last twelve years of his life. Woodward (1962) described this machine:

> It consists of a hollow glass cylinder (7½ in. long by 4½ in. diameter) supported on two wooden uprights. Through it runs a metal bar to which a handle is attached, by means of which the cylinder can be freely rotated. A leather pad (to which is firmly attached a piece of black silk) is pressed against the cylinder. It is controlled, very simply, by a thumbscrew. On an attached platform (8 in. long by 5 in. wide) and mounted on a glass insulating column, is a metal arm with a thin rod (9½ in. long) attached to it, at the end of which is a small metal ball 1 in. in diameter. The whole "machine" is mounted on four glass insulating legs (4½ in. in height).[14]

Presumably, the patient caught hold of the ball and, as the metal arm made contact with the rotating cylinder, received a shock—the intensity depending on the vigor with which the handle was turned.

It is important to note that this was a frictional machine that discharged electric current in one discharge and was not a continuous-current apparatus such as became possible after Alessandro Volta developed the first electric battery in 1799, eight years after Wesley's death. Continuous-current apparati are those used in electroconvulsive shock treatment. This does not mean that it was impossible to administer harmful shocks with friction machines. By storing up current in Leyden jars, which were available to Wesley, it was possible to vary the amount of shock that was administered.

Also, some machines had attached wands with insulated handles that could administer varying amounts of shock dependent on the distance the wand was held from the area of the body toward which it was directed. Current could be built up by turning the handle. More powerful shocks jumped greater distances. As noted earlier, Wesley advised more frequent, weaker shocks and admonished his assistants to be careful not to harm their patients.

The first part of Wesley's *Desideratum* (1760) reviews all the information he could gather on electricity. He asserted, "To throw all the Light I can on the Subject, I subjoin a few Extracts from several other Writers."[15] One of those whose thinking he reviewed was his contemporary J. P. Marat (1743–1793), an eccentric Frenchman who was one of the most influential electrotherapists of the eighteenth century.

Marat distinguished among five methods, three of which Wesley might have used at one time or another. The first method, Marat termed "l'electrisation par bains" in which the patient would sit in an insulated chair and hold one of the conductors of the machine (e.g., the metal ball) while the handle was turned to generate current. As a result, the patient's body was bathed with the warmth of electricity. The second method was a variation of the first and was labeled "l'electrisation par impression de souffle." In this method the conductor was placed on the affected body part, which then received a focused sensation of a gentle, warm breeze. The third method was termed "par frictions." This method did not utilize the machine but, instead, involved rubbing flannel that had been wrapped around the affected part with a metal plate attached to a glass handle. The fourth method, "par etincelles," drew sparks from the affected organ by attaching an uncharged metal wand to the affected body part, which, in turn, was connected to a conductor from the machine. The last method listed by Marat was called "par commotions." In this procedure a strong discharge was sent across the diseased body part. On some occasions this method induced heart attacks, convulsions, blindness, and sometimes death.[16] This is the friction method most akin to later psychiatric electroconvulsive continuous-current shock treatment. It was not used by Wesley.

Although a discussion of the theory of what was going on in these treatments will follow in the next section, it could be stated at this point that there were two basic processes involved in these treatments: attraction and repulsion. It was assumed that the human body was a conductor of electricity and that it would attract current as well as repel it if the body was attached to some other conductive material. In general, it was theorized that where a body part was not functioning or was paralyzed, electricity was deficient and attraction treatment was needed. In this procedure the person was positioned in an insulated chair and then connected to the friction machine by holding on to a metal connection, as in Marat's "l'electrisation par bains" method. On the other hand, it was theorized that where a body part was feverish or infected, electricity was excessive and withdrawal treatment was needed. In this procedure the person was positioned in an insulated chair and then sparks were drawn from the infected part, as in Marat's "par etincelles" approach.

Wesley's Reasoning about Electricity

Primarily, Wesley was a pragmatist. He applied what worked without much attention to explaining causation. He called himself an "experimentalist" but used that term in a far different way from how it is used in modern science. Others called him an "empiric." They were probably more correct. His recommendation of the use of resin for cold sores, as in his *Primitive Physick*, is an example of this approach. Dunlop (1964) noted this discovery: "As he sat beneath a tree and read a book, his tongue worried with a cold sore. A bed of resin fell on his page. Wesley applied it to the sore and effected a cure. From then on he cured other sores in this fashion."[17] So, his application of electric shock to disease and suffering was probably more an artifact of trial and error than of reasoned judgment.

Nevertheless, by the time he wrote his *Desideratum*, Wesley had thought long and hard about the nature of electricity. He provided his readers an extensive justification for thinking of electricity as the elixir of life that God provided to make creation function. Along with Richard Lovett, Wesley speculated that electricity was the source of "all motion in the Universe and that principle in air without which life or flame cannot exist."[18] Lovett, a lay clerk at Worcester Cathedral, wrote a book on electricity four years before Wesley published his volume. Lovett's title speaks of this conviction about the nature of the phenomenon. It was called *The Subtil Medium proved: or the wonderful power of Nature, so long ago Conjectured by the most ancient and remarkable philosophers, which they called sometimes Aether but oftener Elementary Fire, verified: showing that all the distinguishing and essential qualities ascribed to Aether by them and the most eminent modern philosophers, are to be found in Electrical Fire, and that, too, in the utmost decree of perfection.* Lovett felt he had identified the "Materia Subtilis" of Descartes and the essence of Newton's "Aether." Electricity was the "subtle," or integral but unseen, essence of life.

Wesley concurred. His book title *Desideratum* implied that electricity was "the thing to be desired." Wesley called electricity the "soul of the universe." He wrote a chapter explaining that electricity was "the general principle of all Motion in the Universe: From this 'pure Fire,' (which is properly so called) the vulgar 'Culinary Fire' is kindled. For in Truth there is but one Kind of Fire in Nature, which exists in all Places and in all Bodies. And this is subtle and active enough, not only to be, under the Great Cause, the secondary Cause of Motion, but to produce and sustain Life throughout all Nature, as well in Animals as in Vegetables."[19]

Of course, Wesley went beyond Lovett in reasoning theologically that electricity was God given. He stated, "This great machine of the World requires some such constant, active, and powerful Principle, constituted by its Creator, to keep the heavenly Bodies in their several Courses, and at the same Time give Support, Life, and Increase to the various Inhabitants of the Earth."[20]

It should come as no surprise, therefore, to read that he justified the application of electricity for human good as the intent of this creator God. He asserted, "We know that the Creator of the Universe, is likewise, the Governor of all Things therein. But we know likewise, that he governs by second Causes; and that accordingly it is his Will, we should use all the Probable Means he has given us to attain every lawful End."[21]

The "second Causes" in Wesley's statement were the ways, discovered by human investigators, that electricity brought relief from human disease and suffering. He felt these were the laws of God that were intended to be used for "every lawful End."

Wesley's Application of Electricity to Suffering and Illness

In characteristic experimental fashion, Wesley tried electricity first on himself. His cure of his own lameness soon after procuring his first machine has been previously mentioned. His journal records at least two other occasions when he applied this remedy to himself, once when he was seventy years old and once when he was eighty. Hill described these events.[22] In 1773, while on one of his many preaching tours, Wesley had such a pain in his left side and shoulder that he had great difficulty even lifting his hand to his face. He felt that the side/shoulder pain was a result of the earlier inflammation in his throat. After getting one of his assistants to electrify him, he felt much better and was able to preach in the evening. Ten years later he was electrified to relieve leg cramping. Three months earlier he had contracted a cold while riding in an open carriage from one preaching appointment to another. This had resulted in a deep cough that would not dissipate. He tried to keep preaching but became very weak and was put to bed. After a night of rest, coupled with some vomiting, he felt better and set out for another town. Shortly after arrival there, he became feverish and had to lie down. His chest became tight, and he experienced violent cramps in his legs. He convinced a friend to electrify him in the legs and chest several times a day. A few days later he had no more fever, tightness in the chest, or cramps in his legs, and he was able to resume preaching. These examples indicate his personal experience and confidence in the method.

However, it is to Wesley's book *The Desideratum* that we must turn to gain a complete understanding of electrotherapy. After thoroughly surveying the writing and research on electricity that had been done up to that time, Wesley turned in the second half of his book to practical applications. He introduced this section with these words: "I have been hitherto endeavouring to make Electricity plain: I shall endeavour in the second Place, to make it useful."[23] Ascribing, as we might expect, electricity's usefulness to "the wise Author of Nature" (i.e., to God), Wesley contended that it "communicates Activity and Motion to Fluids in general, and particularly accelerates the Motion of the Blood in the human Body. . . . And it is certain many bodily Disorders may be removed, even by this safe and easy Operation."[24] This underlying assumption that electric shock was a stimulant was the primary rationale behind most of Wesley's treatments. So, he based his thinking on the classic humoral theory that goes all the way back to Hippocrates.

After detailing these assumptions, Wesley listed thirty-seven ailments in which "electrification has been found eminently useful." We can probably assume that this was not simply a list of conjectured cures but that, by the time his book was published, treatment of each disorder had actually been attempted. In fact, this list is followed by forty-nine paragraphs, each of which details a case in which the patient was electrified. The paragraphs, while generally positive in their outcomes, do not read as outlandish claims. In no few cases, the treatment is gradual and, in some cases, temporary. Some paragraphs include various reports of treatment. In several situations, such as cancers and tumors, Wesley contended that electrification might have curative powers where no other medicines have been able to help.

Several examples of the cures reported in these paragraphs reveal the type of case material that Wesley depended on to make his judgments.

> Abigail Brown, aged 22, . . . was from a Child frequently afflicted with a violent Head-ache. . . . She was electrified five Days successively, having one Wire applied to the fore Part, another to the hinder Part of the Head, and receiving seven or eight Shocks each Time. Hereby she was entirely cured, nor has found any Pain in her Head since, unless occasionally for want of Sleep.

> . . . Anne Heathcot . . . was seized, in May last, with what is commonly called an "Ague in the Head," having a violent Pain in her Head, Face,

and Teeth. After trying abundance of Remedies, to no purpose, she was, in August, electrified thro' the Head. Immediately the Pain fix'd in her Teeth. She was electrified four Times more, and has felt nothing of it since.

. . . William Jones, a Plaisterer . . . fell from a Scaffold on Thursday, Feb 15 last. He was grievously bruised, both outwardly and inwardly, and lay in violent pain utterly helpless, till Saturday in the Afternoon, when he was brought (carried) by two Men to be electrified. After a few Minutes he walk'd home alone, and on Monday went to work.

. . . A Man, fifty-seven Years old, who had been deaf for thirty-two Years, was so relieved in a few Days, as to hear tolerably well.

. . . A young Lady had been affected with Fits near seven Years, which seized her without any Warning, and threw her flat on her Face, quite insensible. These frequently returned twice in a Day. This was attended with almost continual Coldness in her Feet. Her Stomach also was much affected. She stood upon a Wire coming from the Coat of the Phial, and to complete the Circuit, another Wire was laid upon her Head, by which means the Fire was conveyed to that Part. By this Means both the Fits and Coldness were gradually removed, and a complete Cure effected.

. . . One at Upsal, who had lost the Use of his Limbs from Cold, for several Years, was in some Weeks quite restored.

. . . Sarah Guilford, aged 37, . . . was for upwards of seven Years so afflicted with Rheumatism in her right Side, that the Knee and the Ankle were wasted exceedingly. January 2d last she was electrified, and perfectly cured in one Ray But it threw her into a profuse Sweat, particularly from those Parts which had been most affected.

. . . E - T- taking cold, was seized with a sore Throat, which grew worse and worse for six Days. She then could not swallow even a Bit of Bread soaked in Tea. The same Morning she was electrified, so as to direct the Shock in a right Line thro' the Part affected. By the Time she got home she could eat any Thing. Two shocks more made a perfect Cure.[25]

These examples illustrate the variety of both the methods that were used and the ailments that were treated by electricity during the last half of the eighteenth century. They corroborate Wesley's observation that the majority of the cases were of the nervous, hysteric type. He asserted, "We know it [electricity] is a thousand medicines in one; in particular, that it is the most efficacious medicine in nervous disorders of every kind, which has yet been discovered."[26] It is important to remember, however, that Wesley's rationale for these effects was physiological, not psychological. He concluded, "It seems the Electric Fire in Cases of this kind and of many other Kinds, dilates the minute Vessels, and capillary Passages, as well as separates the clogging Particles of the stagnating Fluids. By accelerating likewise the Motion of the Blood, it removes many Obstructions."[27]

It is interesting to note, however, that not one of the cases recounted by Wesley in *The Desideratum* refers to "the English Malady," or depression. There was a great debate in the eighteenth century about the nature of this disorder. It was so common that the French, among others, contended that the British were peculiarly susceptible to symptoms of morose melancholy. An evaluation of

Britain's poor social conditions and widespread poverty in these years of transition from rural to urban industrial economy might lead us to contend that depression would be largely exogenous not endogenous, environmental rather than temperamental. Such an analysis might explain the curious omission of this disorder from those that Wesley contended might be healed through electrification. He encouraged his followers to be clean, hygienic, honest, frugal, temperate, and compassionate. Perhaps he felt that depression would be cured more in these ways than by electrification. The fact remains, however, that depression was widespread, and it is curious that, with all his concern for health, Wesley made no reference to it in either his book on electrotherapy or his book on general healing.

A final comment on Wesley's approach to electrotherapy needs to be made. It concerns the treatment cautions he recommended. While the cases he reported seem to include the variety of methods noted earlier, in all treatment he advised against haphazard administrations of shock. His words of caution on the next-to-last page of *The Desideratum* are as follows: "In order to prevent any ill Effect, these two cautions should always be remembered. First, let not the Shock be too violent; rather let several small Shocks be given. Secondly, do not give a Shock to the whole Body, when only a particular Part is affected. If it be given to the Part affected only, little Harm can follow even from a violent Shock."[28]

Wesley's Influence on Later Electrotherapy

In the early pages of his book, Wesley proclaimed that he was indebted to Franklin for the speculative part of *The Desideratum* and to Lovett for the practical. Yet in one matter, he strongly disagreed with Lovett. Lovett contended that the use of electricity in treating disease would make no progress until and unless the medical community embraced it. Wesley adamantly disagreed with Lovett on this. He stated that if society had to wait on the physicians to try it, society would wait in vain because physicians were too committed to making money by prescribing complex medications for which they charged much money. According to Wesley, physicians would not be interested in such a simple, cheap treatment as electrification until they "have more regard to the interests of their neighbours than their own. At least not till there are no more apothecaries in the land or till physicians are independent of them."[29]

However, he never gave up hoping they would change. Wesley concluded his book with a somewhat sarcastic plea:

> Before I conclude, I would beg one Thing (if it be not too great a Favour) from the Gentlemen of the Faculty [physicians], and indeed from all who desire Health and Freedom from Pain, either for themselves or their Neighbors. It is,
>
> That none of them would condemn they know not what:
>
> That they would hear the Cause, before they pass Sentence:
>
> That they would not peremptorily pronounce against Electricity, while they know little or nothing about it.
>
> Rather let every candid Man take a little Pains, to understand the Question before he determines it. Let him for two or three Weeks (at least) try it for himself in the above-named Disorders. And then his own Senses will show him, whether it is a mere Play-thing, or the noblest Medicine yet known in the World.[30]

It should be obvious that John Wesley had already concluded the latter. But it must be remembered that he did so on the basis of thorough study of the literature and prolonged reasoning and reflection, coupled with extensive pragmatic application both on himself and on others. His was not an uninformed assessment. While his judgment about the willingness of physicians to utilize electrotherapy turned out to be somewhat overdrawn, his invitation to them to try it before passing judgment cannot be discounted. Turrell, writing more than 175 years later, agreed with Wesley that we "still need some lovers of mankind, who have some knowledge of the animal economy, to be diligent in making experiments on the subject"[31]

Nevertheless, Wesley was not without his critics. Joseph Priestley, the Unitarian minister who wrote one of the definitive books on electricity that Wesley reviewed in his *Desideratum*, declared, "This account of the medical use of electricity by Mr. Lovett and Mr. Wesley is certainly liable to an objection which will always lie against the accounts of these persons, who not being of the faculty [i.e., not being physicians], cannot be supposed capable of distinguishing with accuracy either the nature of the disorder or the consequence of a seeming cure."[32]

Even Benjamin Franklin, who later changed his mind, said in a letter read to the Royal Society in 1758 that he "never knew any permanent advantage from electricity in palsies. . . . Perhaps some permanent advantage might be obtained if the electrical shocks had been accompanied with proper medicine and regimen under the direction of a skilled physician."[33]

Of course, the truth is that Wesley was as well informed and as skilled as many physicians in his day. His two books *The Desideratum* (1760) and *Primitive Physick* (1747) are based on much reading and personal experience. Moreover, the including of treatment for illness in the tasks of clergy had a long-standing tradition in seventeenth- and eighteenth-century England. Many clergy and lords-of-the-manor offered medical treatment to the poor who could not afford physicians. While nineteenth-century Methodism in both England and North America evidenced an increasing differentiation between the roles of clergy and physicians, in Wesley's time this distinction was not necessarily true. In fact, although the free clinics that Wesley started seem to have become defunct soon after his death in 1791, Methodist pastors persisted in offering medical advice to their parishioners well into the 1800s. Further, not all physicians were offended by Wesley's involvement in medical matters. A number of them were prominent in early Methodism.[34]

That electrotherapy was embraced by an increasing number of physicians later in the eighteenth century cannot be denied. A few of these developments were noted in the introduction to this chapter. Among other developments was the first installation of a room for electrification in the asylum at Leicester in 1788. A fascinating account of an electric cure of an epidemic of hysteric reactions in a cotton mill at Lancashire was reported in the *Gentleman's Magazine* in 1787. A physician with a portable electric machine shocked a number of female workers who had gone into convulsions in imitation of a colleague who had a mouse put down her blouse in a playful ruse. The convulsions stopped, and after a week work returned to normal.

Probably the first physician to write a book on the use of electricity in general medicine was Christian Kratzenstein in 1745. By 1783, Nicholas Phillipe Ledru and his son Charles established a "medico-electric" clinic in France and made house calls using a portable machine similar to that of Wesley's. Electricity was being used in Italy and Germany by 1786, when Galvani published his research that led to continuous-current applications. That physicians were willing to have their names in print with Wesley's indicated that electrotherapy was finally accepted. Even Benjamin Franklin had begun offering treatment by this time. Although these developments were, no doubt, due to more than Wesley's initiative, Turrell's evaluation of his efforts would evoke almost universal agreement. He stated, "Clearly, we find [in Wesley] a man of conspicuous ability, of indomitable energy, of reckless and fearless impetuosity, of science and fixed convictions, and of outstanding 'Benevolence to Human Kind.'"[35]

Conclusion

By the mid-nineteenth century, the electrotherapy that Wesley had practiced on a theological and pragmatic basis at last had a firm theoretical and rational foundation. Wesley's heritage can be seen in today's physical therapy where electricity is applied to muscle stimulation and general medicine. This tradition is independent of psychiatry's more extreme application of electricity in electro-convulsive shock treatment. Wesley was much more cautious. Nevertheless, it cannot be denied that Wesley, in his zeal, was convinced that electricity was "the greatest medicine yet known to the world" and might someday be of help in treating every kind of malady.[36] His legacy is great.

6
John Wesley the Spiritualist

The word *spiritualist* is not used here in the typical sense of that word. Of course, John Wesley was a spiritual person, but the word used in this chapter means John Wesley believed strongly in spirits—the good as well as the bad.

Although he was a child of the Enlightenment, Wesley did not follow many educated people in his day in disavowing a belief in the reality of the Devil. He believed Satan could intervene in human affairs and that people could become possessed. Wherever he went in his travels, people told him of telepathy, poltergeist, apparitions, strange events, ghosts, demonic possessions, witchcraft, and dreams. He went out of his way to investigate these accounts. He wrote about many of them in his journal and in the *Arminian Magazine*, which he founded.

Interestingly, Wesley never reported any of these experiences as happening to him personally. While he did believe in supernatural guidance and in demonic involvement in human decisions, he did not sense satanic intrusion into his own life. Yet he was seriously impacted by something that happened in his own home at

Epworth while he was a boy away at school. He heard the story
of Old Jeffery again and again as he was growing up and became
convinced that the Devil was involved. Wesley reported this event
in the *Arminian Magazine*:

> When I was very young I heard several letters read,
> wrote to my elder brother by my father, giving an
> account of strange disturbances, which were in his
> house at Epworth, in Lincolnshire.
>
> When I went down thither, in the year 1720,
> I carefully enquired into the particulars. I spoke to
> each of the persons who were then in the house, and
> took down what each could testify of his or her
> knowledge. The sum of which was this:
>
> On December 2, 1716, while Robert Brown, my
> father's servant, was sitting with one of the maids
> a little before ten at night in the dining-room, which
> opened into the garden, they both heard knocking
> at the door. Robert rose and opened it, but could
> see nobody. Quickly it knocked again and groaned.
> "It is Mr. Turpine," said Robert. "He has the
> stone, and uses to groan so." He opened the
> door again twice or thrice, the knocking being
> twice or thrice repeated. But still seeing nothing,
> and being a little startled, they rose and went to
> bed.
>
> When Robert came to the top of the garret
> stairs he saw a hand-mill, which was at a little
> distance, whirled about very swiftly. When he re-
> lated all this he said, "Nought vexed me but that
> it was empty. I thought if it had been full of malt
> he might have ground out his heart for me." When
> he was in bed he heard, as it were, the gobbling

of a turkey-cock close to the bedside; and soon after the sound of one stumbling over his shoes and boots, but there were none there; he had left them below. The next day he and the maid related these things to the other maid, who laughed heartily and said, "What a couple of fools are you! I defy anything to fright me."

After churning in the evening she put the butter in the tray, and had no sooner carried it into the dairy than she heard a knocking on the shelf where several puncheons of milk stood, first above the shelf, then below; she took the candle and searched both above and below; but being able to find nothing, threw down butter, tray, and all, and ran away for life.

The next evening, between five and six o'clock, my sister Molly, then about twenty years of age, sitting in the dining-room reading, heard as it were the door that led into the hall open and a person walking in, that seemed to have on a silk nightgown, rustling and trailing along. It seemed to walk round her, then to the door, then round again; but she could see nothing. She thought, "It signifies nothing to run away; for whatever it is, it can run faster than me." Presently a knocking began under the table. She took the candle and looked, but could find nothing. Then the iron casement began to clatter and the lid of a warming-pan. Next the latch of the door moved up and down without ceasing. She started up, leaped into her bed without undressing, pulled the bed-clothes over her head, and never ventured to look up till next morning.

A night or two after, my sister Hetty, a year younger than my sister Molly, was waiting as usual, between nine and ten, to take away my father's candle, when she heard someone coming down the garret stairs, walking slowly by her, then going down the best stairs, then up the back stairs, and up the garret stairs. And at every step it seemed the house shook from top to bottom. Just then my father knocked. She went in, took his candle, and got to bed as fast as possible. She told this to my eldest sister in the morning, who told her, "You know, I believe none of these things. Pray let me take away the candle to-night and I will find out the trick."

She accordingly took my sister Hetty's place, and had no sooner taken away the candle than she heard a noise below. She hastened downstairs to the hall where the noise was. But it was then in the kitchen. She ran into the kitchen, where it was drumming on the inside of the screen. When she went round it was drumming on the outside, and so always on the side opposite to her. Then she heard a knocking at the back kitchen door. She ran to it, unlocked it softly, and when the knocking was re-peated, suddenly opened it; but nothing was to be seen. As soon as she had shut it the knocking began again; she opened it again, but could see nothing; when she went to shut the door it was violently thrust against her; she let it fly open, but nothing appeared. She went again to shut it, and it was again thrust against her; but she set her knee and her shoulder to the door, forced it to, and turned the key. Then the knocking began again; but she let it go on, and went up to bed. However, from that time she was thoroughly convinced that there was no imposture in the affair.

The next morning my sister, telling my mother what had happened, she said, "If I hear anything myself, I shall know how to judge." Soon after she begged her to come into the nursery. She did, and heard in the corner of the room, as it were, the violent rocking of a cradle, but no cradle had been there for some years. She was convinced it was preternatural, and earnestly prayed it might not disturb her in her own chamber at the hours of retirement; and it never did. She now thought it was proper to tell my father. But he was extremely angry, and said, "Suky, I am ashamed of you; these boys and girls frighten one another, but you are a woman of sense and should know better. Let me hear of it no more."

At six in the evening he had family prayers as usual. When he began the prayer for the king, a knocking began all round the room, and a thundering knock attended the "Amen." The same was heard from this time every morning and evening while the prayer for the king was repeated. As both my father and mother are now at rest and incapable of being pained thereby, I think it my duty to furnish the serious reader with a key to this circumstance.

The year before King William died my father observed my mother did not say "Amen" to the prayer for the king. She said she could not, for she did not believe the Prince of Orange was king. He vowed he would never cohabit with her till she did. He then took his horse and rode away, nor did she hear anything of him for a twelvemonth. He then came back and lived with her as before. But I fear his vow was not forgotten before God.

Being informed that Mr. Hoole, the vicar of Haxey (an eminently pious and sensible man), could give me some further information, I walked over to him. He said, "Robert Brown came over to me and told me your father desired my company. When I came he gave me an account of all that had happened, particularly the knocking during family prayer. But that evening (to my great satisfaction) we had no knocking at all. But between nine and ten a servant came in and said, 'Old Ferries is coming' (that was the name of one that died in the house), 'for I hear the signal.' This they informed us was heard every night about a quarter before ten. It was toward the top of the house on the outside, at the north-east corner, resembling the loud creaking of a saw, or rather that of a windmill when the body of it is turned about in order to shift the sails to the wind.

"We then heard a knocking over our heads, and Mr. Wesley, catching up a candle, said, 'Come, sir, you shall now hear for yourself.' We went upstairs, he with much hope, and I (to say the truth) with much fear. When we came into the nursery it was knocking in the next room; when we were there it was knocking in the nursery. And there it continued to knock, though we came in, particularly at the head of the bed (which was of wood) in which Miss Hetty and two of her younger sisters lay. Mr. Wesley, observing that they were much affected, though asleep, sweating and trembling exceedingly, was very angry, and, pulling out a pistol, was going to fire at the place from whence the sound came. But I catched him by the arm and said, 'Sir, you are convinced this is something preternatural. If so, you cannot hurt it, but you give it power to hurt you.' He then went close to the place and said sternly, 'Thou deaf and dumb devil, why dost thou frighten these children that cannot answer for themselves? Come to me to my study that am a man!' Instantly it knocked his knock (the particular knock which he always used at the gate) as if it would shiver the board in pieces, and we heard nothing more that night."

Till this time my father had never heard the least disturbance in his study. But the next evening, as he attempted to go into this study (of which none had any key but himself), when he opened the door it was thrust back with such violence as had like to have thrown him down. However, he thrust the door open and went in. Presently there was knocking, first on one side, then on the other, and after a time in the next room, wherein my sister Nancy was.

He went into that room, and (the noise continuing) adjured it to speak; but in vain. He then said,

"These spirits love darkness; put out the candle, and perhaps it will speak." She did so, and he repeated his adjuration; but still there was only knocking, and no articulate sound. Upon this he said, "Nancy, two Christians are an overmatch for the devil. Go all of you downstairs; it may be when I am alone he will have courage to speak." When she was gone a thought came in and he said, "If thou art the spirit of my son Samuel, I pray, knock three knocks and no more." Immediately all was silence, and there was no more knocking at all that night.

I asked my sister Nancy (then about fifteen years old) whether she was not afraid when my father used that adjuration? She answered she was sadly afraid it would speak when she put out the candle; but she was not at all afraid in the daytime, when it walked after her, as she swept the chambers, as it constantly did, and seemed to sweep after her. Only she thought it might have done it for her, and saved her the trouble. By this time all my sisters were so accustomed to these noises that they gave them little disturbance. A gentle tapping at their bed head usually began between nine and ten at night. They then commonly said to each other, "Jeffery is coming, it is time to go to sleep." And if they heard a noise in the day and said to my youngest sister, "Hark, Kezzy, Jeffery is knocking above," she would run upstairs, and pursue it from room to room, saying she desired no better diversion.

A few nights after, my father and mother were just gone to bed, and the candle was not taken away, when they heard three blows, and a second, and a third three, as it were with a large oaken staff, struck upon a chest which stood by the bedside. My father immediately arose, put on his nightgown, and hearing great noises below took the candle and went down; my mother walked by his side. As they went down the broad stairs they heard as if a vessel full of silver was poured upon my mother's breast and ran jingling down to her feet. Quickly after there was a sound, as if a large iron ball was thrown among many bottles under the stairs; but nothing was hurt.

Soon after, our large mastiff dog came and ran to shelter himself between them. While the disturbances continued he used to bark and leap, and snap on one side and the other, and that frequently before any person in the room heard any noise at all. But after two or three days he used to tremble and creep away before the noise began. And by this the family knew it was at hand, nor did the observation ever fail. A little before my father and mother came into the hall it seemed as if a very large coal was violently thrown upon the floor and dashed all to pieces, but nothing was seen. My father then cried out, "Suky, do you not hear? All the pewter is thrown about the kitchen." But when they looked all the pewter was in its place.

Then there was a loud knocking at the back door. My father opened it, but saw nothing. It was then at the front door. He opened that, but it was still lost labour. After opening first the one and then the other several times he turned and went up to bed.

But the noises were so violent all over the house that he could not sleep till four in the morning.

Several gentlemen and clergymen now earnestly advised my father to quit the house. But he constantly answered, "No, let the devil flee from me; I will never flee from the devil." But he wrote to my eldest brother at London to come down. He was preparing to do so when another letter came, informing him that the disturbances were over, after they had continued (the latter part of the time day and night) from the 2nd of December to the end of January.[1]

The letters and journal notes kept by Wesley's father and mother coupled with Wesley's own interview notes may make these months of poltergeist in the Epworth parsonage one of the fullest accounts of such events that are known. The records of Old Jeffery's visits are phenomenal. Jacob Priestly concluded that these accounts were "perhaps the best authenticated and best told story of the kind that is anywhere extant."[2] However, while a number of the letters were written by Wesley's sisters, there are no extant accounts written by Hetty—the sister who is described as most involved.

Initially, everyone heard the strange sounds except Wesley's father, Samuel. It was commonly thought that when a person did not hear what others were hearing, it meant something foreboding—like some evil would befall him or her. The other family members hesitated to tell him what they were hearing, but the sounds became so frequent they decided he should know. At first he joined Mrs. Wesley in thinking that one of the daughters' boyfriends was playing tricks on them or that rats had caused the disturbances. They also wondered if some parishioners who did not like the Wesleys were trying to get them to leave. He soon became convinced, however, that the sounds had a supernatural, even demonic, cause. They became concerned that the message of the sounds meant that their oldest son, Samuel Jr., was in danger of suffering a violent death. They were greatly relieved when they heard he was safe and sound. The only logic that ever came of these strange sounds was that time when the knocks became louder and more repetitive during the prayers of Samuel Sr. for the king.[3]

On two occasions the *presence* was confronted. As Wesley's account noted, his father got a pistol and was about to fire in the direction of the sounds but was constrained. Then he sternly ordered the sounds to be limited to his study instead of frightening his children. When the sounds did come to his study the next night, he ordered it to speak—to no avail.

The sisters came to the place where they found the noises harmless and humorous. Emilia gave it the name of Old Jeffery—a curious goblin who, although irritating, was basically harmless. When Mrs. Wesley blew a horn that she believed would scare rats away, the sisters protested that if Old Jeffery meant no harm, he might become troublesome if the sound of the horn hurt his ears.

John Wesley never fully agreed with his sisters, however. He remained convinced that Old Jeffery with his knockings in all areas of the house, rumblings above and below stairs, clattering of bottles, footsteps at all hours of the night, sounds of dancing in empty rooms where the doors were locked—all were somehow visitations of evil forces. He spent a great deal of energy trying unsuccessfully to tease out the meaning of the events. He retold the extensive story of Old Jeffery as a forewarning of the danger all persons face of being visited by supernatural evil spirits.

Wesley once commented that he believed in spirits because he believed the Bible.[4] He said he would give up his belief in the Devil, for example, when he ceased to believe the Bible. While he thought that the giving of spiritual gifts had degenerated after the third century, the deliverance ministry was needed in every age. He claimed that "as long as Satan is the god of this world," so long would prayers for deliverance be needed.[5]

This conviction led Wesley to go out of his way to investigate stories of spirit involvement in his travels. People knew he had a deep interest in the spirit world. He would often stay a day after his preaching to follow up stories told to him by his listeners. His journal records a number of visitations he made. In addition he often preached about the need for people to be on guard against evil spirits. There was significant opposition to his emphasis on these issues, but he often wrote of persons overcoming their objections when they experienced deliverance. He gave the example of a Calvinistic Quaker who was delivered. He wrote, "One John Haydon, a 'Church man' highly critical of deliverance, was over powered by the presence of God and demons manifested themselves. He cried out, 'O thou devil! Thou cursed devil! Yea, thou legion of devils! Thou canst not stay. Christ will cast thee out. I know his work has begun.'"[6]

Once while Wesley was traveling along one of the roads outside London, he overtook a man who wanted to talk. This man shared his strong negative opinions about the deliverance teachings of a preacher named John Wesley. When he finished his criticism, he asked whether his fellow traveler agreed. Wesley, who had remained silent, felt he had to respond. He answered, "Sir, I am John Wesley." The embarrassed man hurried on off without saying another word.[7]

Conclusion

In summary, John Wesley was a spiritualist in the sense that he strongly believed in both good and bad spirits that were active in

the lives of people. He studied seriously the story of the visits of
Old Jeffery to his family home and cautioned his followers to be
on guard of being visited by evil sprits and becoming possessed. He
considered the ministry of deliverance from spirits to be central to
his mission.

7

John Wesley the Romantic

The romantic endeavors of John Wesley were replete with failure. Although he had periodic and clearly identifiable amorous feelings throughout his life, his vocational commitment, coupled with a profound timidity, resulted in a hesitant style of expressing romantic inclinations. Only at middle age did he finally marry, and that relationship was so tumultuous that they separated. This sometimes assertive, often reticent, always desirous, strangely independent way of relating to the opposite sex is yet another of Wesley's eccentric traits that underlay his public persona.

There is no doubt that Wesley stands out from among other noteworthy Christian leaders as one who wrote about his romantic experiences and the theological struggles he had with them. He persistently and overtly sought God's will in this area of his life. Yet strangely enough, he recommended that the leaders of the classes he organized on his evangelistic journeys remain single rather than get married. He did not base this recommendation on disapproval of amorous relationships, however. His reasoning was that his preachers might be saddled with children who might misbehave and disrupt the ministry. This chapter reflects on Wesley's romantic experiences with women throughout his life: (1) at Oxford his attraction to Betty Kirkham and Mary Pendarves, (2) in Georgia his courtship of Sophie Hopkey, (3) at Newcastle his relationship with Grace Murray, and (4) in London his marriage to Molly Vazeille.

Betty Kirkham and Mary Pendarves

Wesley graduated from Christ Church College, Oxford, and returned as a teaching fellow of Greek and Hebrew to Lincoln College soon after his ordination to the priesthood in the Church of England in 1725. He remained in this position, which required that he be unmarried, until 1736 at which time he accepted the invitation to become the chaplain of Georgia, a new settlement in North America. During his Oxford years, both as student and teacher, he cultivated the habits of self-discipline and stern judgments that were to characterize him throughout his life. Coming out of the small-town rectory at Epworth, where his father was a priest, he was appalled at the depravity and corruption of Oxford—both within the university as well as in the city. Taking his cues for living primarily from his mother, Suzanna, he adopted strict rules for his personal life and became a classic scholar with skills in Hebrew, Greek, and Latin—subjects he was to later teach. He was described as having "the power of concentration, joy in mental exercise for its own sake, self-confidence and a cool imperviousness to the temptations of idleness, pleasure or vice."[1]

Although overly serious about religious duties and very limited in financial resources during this period of his life, Wesley remained attentive to his appearance and was known as a "cheerful companion, much liked for his even temper and air of breeding; neat and exquisitely clean in his person; . . . his features never lost their infantile delicacy. . . . To save the expenses of a barber . . . he wore his own hair long; it was an auburn-brown colour, parted in the middle, smoothly brushed and curling at the ends."[2]

Although not as physically attractive as his brother Charles, John was known as a good conversationalist and loyal friend. Among his acquaintances was Robert Kirkham, one of the members of the Holy Club that John led. John would often spend weekends with the Kirkham family in Gloucestershire, where Robert's father was the rector. Robert hoped that John would marry his sister Betty someday.

John, however, did not have marriage on his mind, even though he thoroughly enjoyed the companionship of women and they, in turn, found him especially attractive because of his neatness and charm. His budding preference for the single life was reinforced by the realization that if he married he would lose his fellowship at Oxford. Wesley came to call Betty Kirkham "dear Varanese." He spent many pleasant Sunday afternoons on the rectory lawn in innocent flirtation and religious conversation. She was eager to hear and willing to learn of his latest thinking about holy living—the topic of conversation at the meetings of Holy Club back at the university. It was a delicious friendship that might have eventually led to marriage had not Betty been wooed by another suitor whom she decided to marry—much to John's dismay, according to his journal.

However, yet another friendship developed between Wesley and a frequent visitor to the Kirkhams, Mary Pendarves, a young widow. Described as "lovely, fashionable, artificial and cultured," she represented all that was most superficially attractive in the aristocracy of the time and was far more cool, brilliant, and seductive than any other woman whom Wesley had ever met.[3] Wesley became intrigued with her willingness to listen to his admonitions and recommendations for devout and disciplined life. It was like a Holy Club away from Oxford. Wesley urged her to get up early, set aside times for prayer, avoid Sunday concerts, and read good books.

He engaged in a parlor game, popular at that time, of giving others pseudoclassical nicknames. "Aspasia" was the name Wesley assigned to Pendarves. Wesley was dazzled by the interaction. Although he hardly knew her, outside infrequent weekends together at the Kirkhams', Wesley fell in love with the ephemeral, gossamer Aspasia, who leaned on him for instruction and said that she saw the "beauty of holiness" in him. They wrote often and expressed themselves in languishing, provocative ways that came close to avowed love. She, however, became drawn into a relationship in London, and Wesley could never admit that his feelings were anything more than concern for her soul. Yet his ponderings suggest it was something more. His commitment to the activities of the Holy Club at Oxford consumed more and more of his energy as an unmarried parson. He could not realistically conceive of a marriage that would distract him from these activities. So his time at Oxford left him with amorous emotions that he could only minimally admit. However, this was to change, as we shall see when Wesley went to North America.

Sophie Hopkey

In the spring of 1735 John and his brother Charles made the fateful journey to Epworth to be with their father, who was dying. Soon after his death the brothers felt obliged to crown their father's life work, a commentary on the book of Job coauthored with Johnny Whitelambe, by presenting it to the queen. While waiting for their audience with the queen, Wesley was introduced to Colonel James Oglethorpe, a soldier of some distinction who had been instrumental in helping to found the settlement of Georgia in the New World. Samuel, John's father, had thought highly of Oglethorpe and had written two poems in his honor as well as donated money to his causes. On this basis, Oglethorpe offered John and Charles the opportunity to go to Georgia with him. They accepted his offer. Charles would be secretary to Oglethorpe and John would be chaplain of Georgia, with his primary duty as vicar of the parish church in Savannah.

Because of the malaise into which the Holy Club had deteriorated and his own self-doubt and reflection about his own salvation after the death of his father, John accepted the offer. He left his fellowship at Oxford and embarked for Georgia aboard the *Simmonds* on October 14, 1735. Wesley wrote that his chief motive in going was to save his own soul and to convert the Indians. However, both these intentions were undermined by a somewhat problematic romantic relationship with Sophie Hopkey.

Wesley became aware that, while his saintliness and strict observance of the sacraments provoked displeasure among the general populace, his attraction to some of the women of the settlement increased. When Charles left to accompany Oglethorpe to Frederica, a hundred miles to the south, John wrote him, "I stand in jeopardy every hour, because of young, refined, God-fearing women. . . . Pray that I know none of them after the flesh."[4] Of peculiar temptation in this regard was Sophie Hopkey, the niece of an unpopular store owner.

When Wesley first met her, Miss Hopkey had recently suffered through a thwarted love affair with one of the clerks at the store who had threatened to harm her if she abandoned him. Her uncle, Mr. Causton, put Wesley in charge of her spiritual condition. He began to lead her in Bible study and to give her lessons in French. In his efforts to console her, Wesley learned that she did not want to marry the former store clerk and that she was unsure of her own salvation. With Wesley's lack of understanding of his own proclivities, this set up a situation in which he became romantically attracted to Sophie during the time he was instructing her on religious matters.

Sophie Hopkey was eighteen years old, attractive, charming, pious, and coy. Wesley took great interest in her welfare and seemed oblivious to the gossip his attentions were causing among the citizens of Savannah. They met daily—usually at his rectory. She demurely inquired of Wesley's companions what color of dress Reverend Wesley most admired and, subsequently, routinely arrived at his door in flowing white muslin apparel. During the week and every Sunday, Wesley invited Sophie to his house for "further instruction."[5] Wesley read to her from the Christian classics and reported she was "all stillness and attention."

She had qualities that appealed deeply to Wesley. He described her as "a girl whose 'soul appeared to be wholly made of mildness, gentleness, longsuffering' who was 'all sympathy, tenderness, compassion,' yet who preserved 'in all that yielding easiness a modesty pure as light.'"[6] He began to fantasize about a romantic relationship with her. To add to her attractiveness, she owned property that Wesley began to realize might offer him some security.

Over time, Wesley became deeply involved with Hopkey. He fell in love with her but fought the feeling out of his long-standing conviction that he should remain single and not become burdened with family obligations that might interfere with his availability to act on God's call on his life. He would have disengaged himself from the relationship in light of this conviction about marriage except for the fact that she had assured him that she, too, was not interested in marriage but considered the single life essential for Christian dedication. Their relationship became more involved quite apart from their protestations.

However, a situation developed that was to color every other serious relationship with women Wesley was to have throughout his life—he became physically sick and needed someone to nurse him back to health. Sophie volunteered. This nurse-patient paradigm established a unique type of relationship. He began to admit to himself his romantic feeling toward Sophie.

Sophie's uncle—Wesley's closest friend—and General Oglethorpe advised Wesley to marry and settle down in Georgia, but Wesley was tormented by ambivalence. He would almost propose marriage and then pull back. Unfortunately, both Sophie and Wesley were reticent to boldly state their feelings.

In an effort to resolve Wesley's hesitation, his friend Charles Delamotte arranged for him to draw one of three slips of paper out of a hat. On the slips were these statements: Marry; Think not of it this year; and Think not of it no more. Wesley pulled out the last statement and felt God had spoken. When Sophie came to see him, she found that he had left a note for her and had gone walking in the woods. The note read, "I find, Miss Sophie, I can't take fire in my bosom and not be burned."[7] She correctly interpreted this that he did not want to pursue a love relationship any further. She was devastated because she, too, was convinced that she loved him.

Some time thereafter, Wesley learned that Sophie had accepted the proposal of another of Causton's clerks, Thomas Williamson—a man Wesley considered plain, stupid, and not religious. Wesley asked her whether she really wanted to marry Williamson. She gave Wesley one more chance by replying, "Sir, I have given Mr. Williamson my consent unless you have anything to object to." Again, Wesley hesitated. Williamson moved with dispatch, and the marriage was finalized very quickly.

At this turn of events, Wesley became enraged. Sophie no longer came for instruction, nor did she continue to ask for his advice. He was beside himself with frustration and anger. He began to accost her verbally for her lack of seriousness about being a Christian. He even went so far as to refuse Holy Communion to

Sophie and her new husband. Williamson issued a writ of slander against Wesley, and Wesley was arrested.

Although the grand jury acquitted him on the basis of the issue being a religious matter, by this time Wesley had made up his mind to leave Georgia and return to England. He posted his intentions on the church door and slipped away to Charleston in the middle of the night—a dejected, forlorn man.

This failure in the relationship with Sophie Hopkey combined with a lack of success in both converting the Indians and gaining parish support from the settlers probably provoked the depressive mental state that plagued Wesley when he returned to London in the early spring of 1738. It set the stage for the "heart strangely warmed experience" that occurred during the Moravian prayer meeting on Aldersgate Street, May 24, 1738.

Grace Murray

More than three years after his Aldersgate experience had propelled him into the preaching missions that were to consume the rest of his life, Wesley published the first of two pamphlets on singleness. In *Thoughts on Marriage and the Single Life* (1741) Wesley wrote that he had often been asked whether the married or unmarried state was preferred. He stated that the single life was best for believers "and, in fact, was required of them."[8] He was but stating in print a position he had advocated since his Oxford days. It was also one that he was sorely tempted to abandon in Georgia with Sophie Hopkey and one he was destined to explicitly forsake later in a relationship with Grace Murray.

Nevertheless, Wesley's opinion was that Scripture mandated that believers become "eunuchs" for the sake of the gospel. He met with converts all over the British Isles and urged them to remain single after they became Christians. Celibacy, Wesley contended, was what Jesus wanted, and God would give the gift of continence to those who dedicated themselves to him. In a later pamphlet on the issue, published in 1765, he moderated his views about marriage to some degree but still insisted that single persons could serve God without distraction, could avoid loving one person too much, and needed to accumulate no wealth.[9]

Of course, Wesley had to face the fact that many of those in his Society were already married or had difficulty controlling their sexual desires. He recommended the married remain bound together. They should be willing to satisfy the needs of their spouses. He also recognized that getting married was to be preferred over promiscuity—a state Wesley interpreted as being weak and losing the gift of continence. Wesley disagreed strongly with the Moravians, who came to have a positive outlook on sexual relations in general. Marriage was definitely, in his mind, a less-preferred alternative to singleness. He rarely performed weddings or attended those of his members performed by parish priests. Of the four that he mentioned in his writings, one was that of his brother Charles, a wedding he could hardly avoid.

Overall, Wesley's followers tolerated but did not follow his teachings on singleness. Many married. A number of the former members of the Holy Club, including Charles, had wives by the time Wesley began a relationship with Grace Murray in the late 1740s. At this time the Methodist movement was in full swing. Not only had Class Meetings been formed, but also several schools and orphanages had been established.

Grace Murray was in charge of the Methodist Orphanage at Newcastle. Wesley admired her work but only came into personal contact with her when he, during an illness, was taken to the orphanage for recuperation. Grace, a sailor's widow who had spent much of her early life as a domestic servant, knew well how to nurse a sick person back to health. As in the case of Sophie Hopkey,

Wesley was vulnerable to the care he received. A permanent relationship became feasible. "John did not see why he could not now take to himself a sweet submissive companion who would be a good nurse and housekeeper and accompany him on his incessant travels, assisting him in the work of salvation and ministering to the poor."[10]

Wesley overcame his ambivalence about singleness as well as the class difference between them (she was a domestic; he was an Oxford-trained cleric). He proposed and she accepted. "This is too great a blessing for me. I can't tell how to believe it. This is all I could have wished for under Heaven!" Grace exuded. But then Wesley's old habit of indecision set in. Instead of marrying her forthwith, he set off on one of his journeys with her as nurse, secretary, and servant, but not as wife. Wesley was effusive in his adulation of Grace. He wrote in his journal that she was "undeniably the most usefull woman in ye Kingdom. . . . Shew me one in all ye English Annals, whom God so employ'd in so high a degree. I might say, In all ye History of the Church, from ye Death of our Lord to this day."[11]

However, things were not as clear cut as they might have seemed. When they reached Derbyshire, Wesley left her in charge of one of the schools while he returned to London. There she renewed an acquaintance with John Bennet, a fellow Methodist whom she had also nursed to health some time before. Grace changed her mind about Wesley and sent him a note saying she and Bennet had decided to wed. Having overcome his timidity, Wesley asserted himself more than once during the following weeks. Grace went back and forth in her intentions between Bennet and Wesley.

Unfortunately for John, another process was going on that interrupted his relationship with Grace. It was led by his brother Charles, who felt that a marriage between Wesley and a former domestic would detract significantly from the future of the Methodist movement. He listened to one of the sisters in the movement who told him that if John married Grace all the Societies would dissolve. Charles confronted Wesley with this dire possibility. Wesley was not to be outdone. Quite apart from his earlier conviction about singleness, he told Charles, "I have scriptural reason to marry—I know no person so proper as this." He said he did not mind the fact that she was a former domestic servant. He insisted that she had the virtues he needed in a wife. "She was meek, frugal but not sordid, had much common sense, was patient, tender, clean, and quick. Her behavior was engaging and her temper serious, mild, sprightly, and cheerful. She had unparalleled gifts for usefulness among the female members of the flock."[12]

Charles was not to be deterred. He went to Grace and cried, "Grace Murray, you have broken my heart." Charles fell back in a swoon—a behavior he was to repeat some time later when he heard of Wesley's marriage to Molly Vazeille. Through the efforts of Charles and others, Grace and Bennet were married soon thereafter, and John was told about it after the fact. A meeting ensued among the four—John, Charles, Bennet, and Grace. They all embraced and declared the marriage the will of God.

Unlike the anger that overwhelmed him when Sophie Hopkey married another man, Wesley became disconsolate and reproachful toward both Grace's new husband as well as his brother Charles. He deeply felt the loss. He wrote to a friend, "Since I was six years old I never met with such a severe trial as for some time past; for ten years God has been preparing a fellow-labourer for me by a wonderful train of Providence. Last year I was convinced of it. Therefore I delayed not, but we were soon after torn asunder by a whirlwind."[13] John and Grace did not see each other again until they were elderly.

Molly Vazeille

The major thesis of Abelove's book *The Evangelist of Desire: John Wesley and the Methodists* (1990) is that Wesley's influence was primarily based on "deference"—a style of subservience that both cultivated and encouraged others. Rarely, if ever, had the common people, to whom his ministry appealed, had contact with a cleric whose appearance and demeanor commanded such attention. Wesley always appeared in black clerical garb with white Geneva tabs for a collar. He never wore a wig. His long, light brunette hair was always parted, brushed, and meticulously combed. One man, who intended to accost him, stopped and fell back, struck, as he said, by Wesley's hair and dress. His complexion remained soft and smooth, even to his death. All in all, he was an imposing figure who called for respect.

Likewise, however, his demeanor called forth affection and adoration. The adulation seen in Betty, Mary, Sophie, and Grace was but a foretaste of what was to come as Wesley traveled across Scotland, Wales, England, and Ireland throughout the last half of the eighteenth century. Men respected him; women adored him. He spent many hours, satisfying both to himself and to others, talking with people about their lives. Females were deeply attracted to him and he to them. However, Wesley always maintained his composure despite the temptation toward indiscretion. He wrote in his journal of the struggle he sometimes faced. He stated that he constantly prayed to remain pure in thought and deed.

He continued to write about the advantages of the single life. Interestingly, his second pamphlet, *Thoughts on a Single Life*, was published fourteen years after his own marriage. In it he stated that his ideas were "just the same as they had been for the previous thirty years, and the same as they must be, unless I give up the Bible."[14] We may wonder whether his thoughts were not, to a significant degree, colored by the unhappiness he experienced in his marriage to Molly Vazeille.

Of even greater interest is the fact that the marriage in 1751 occurred only six months after he lost Grace Murray to John Bennet. Wesley explained his marriage on the basis of defending the movement against the scandalous accusations of many that Wesley, as well as many of his unmarried leaders, were engaging in sexual indiscretions. Wesley said the Methodist movement did not need to defend against such slander, so he took a wife. However, we might conjecture that he was marrying on the rebound from the loss of Grace Murray. Ayling (1979) contended this was the case. He wrote, "He [Wesley] had always demanded feminine companionship, and at the age of forty-seven wanted something more durably satisfying than the pious intimacies of confession and counsel which he was forever exchanging with the Methodist sisters. He had always been both attentive and attractive to women. Meeting countless people year in year out, busy among a thousand friends and fellow labourers meant he could still at bottom be lonely."[15] This is probably the truth, but it is intriguing that he still asserted the value of singleness at the very time he was married.

Molly Vazeille was very active in the London Class Meeting. She was the well-to-do widow of a successful merchant and the mother of four children. Wesley often spent the cold winter months in London at his apartment at the Foundery on City Road. Wesley and Vazeille's courtship developed during the fall and winter of 1750–51, four years after the death of Molly's husband. The couple signed a marriage agreement on February 9, 1751, that guaranteed that Wesley would not touch her personal fortune, nor would she be responsible for his debts. No specific date for the wedding was set at that time.

When notified of his brother's forthcoming marriage, Charles Wesley, who had never approved of John getting married, wrote in his journal, "I was thunderstruck, and could only answer that he had given me the first blow. . . . I refused his company to the chapel and retired to mourn with my faithful Sally [his wife]."[16] Charles jealously guarded the reputation of the movement against indiscretion and was afraid that marriage would result in too much strain due to John's many travels—a fear that was well warranted because of what transpired in John's marriage to Molly.

Nevertheless, the marriage was consummated on February 18, 1751, when John was forty-seven years old. By 1758 Molly had left him—unable to cope with her feelings of jealousy over the adulation of Wesley's many admirers who sought his counsel on his travels. He had written numerous love letters to her in the early marriage, among them the following: "I wonder at myself. How is it that absence does not lesson but increase my affection. I feel you every day nearer to my heart."[17]

Wesley became concerned as early as three months after marriage over Molly's uneasiness. He wrote, "My wife, upon all supposition that I did not love her, and that I trusted others more than her, had often fretted herself almost to death."[18] Sadly, her feelings did not dissipate, and she left Wesley on many occasions, the last being in 1758. Some thirteen years after the separation, he wrote in his journal, "I did not desert her, I did not send her away, I will not ask her to return." And a decade later, upon his return from the Isle of Wight, Wesley learned that Molly had died four days earlier.

Conclusion

In these five relationships (two in Oxford, one each in Georgia and Newcastle, and a final one in London) we see yet another unique feature of the life of John Wesley. Each in a slightly different way shows his humanity and style that, in one sense, are but traits of many who become consumed with a vocation but, in another sense, reveal the dynamics of loneliness. Wesley is one of the few religious leaders who filtered these interactions through the dynamics of his faith. In his reflections that appear in his writing, we see him reasoning about the will of God for him in each of these romantic bonds yet showing very human reactions in their failure.

8

John Wesley the Abolitionist

John Wesley died March 2, 1791, at ten o'clock in the morning. He was eighty-seven years old. Some fourteen months earlier Wesley had written in his journal, "I am an old man, decayed from head to foot. My eyes are dim; my right hand shakes much; my mouth is hot and dry every morning; I have a lingering fever almost every day; my motion is weak and slow. However, blessed be God, I do not slack my labour. I can still preach and write still."[1]

Truer words were never spoken. Up until a week before his death, Wesley kept writing. His last letter, written February 24, 1791, is one that is held in high esteem by those of his followers who have decried that slavery ever existed. This was the letter written to William Wilberforce—a member of the House of Commons who was attempting to have slavery abolished in the British empire. The letter included the following admonition: "O be not weary in well doing! Go on, in the name of God and in the power of His might, till even American slavery (the vilest that ever saw the sun) shall vanish before it."[2]

It would be erroneous, however, to assume that letter reflected only another social issue of which Wesley became aware toward the end of his life. Wesley's concern over slavery in America went back as far as his sojourn in Georgia in the 1730s and his volume entitled *Thoughts upon Slavery*, which was published in 1774.

In 1735 when the Wesley brothers sailed for Georgia, John had stated that he was going to the New World to preach to the "heathens." However, he did not envision that this would mean he would preach to Negro slaves. The 1732 charter to Georgia decreed that every person residing in or born in the province would be free. And a subsequent regulation indicated that Georgians were prohibited from the importation and use of "Black Slaves or Negroes."[3] The Wesleys applauded these charter regulations.

Yet their lack of firsthand acquaintance with slavery was short lived. The brothers made a trip to Charleston in the summer of 1736. Slavery was a part of South Carolina life. Charles wrote in his journal of three incidents that shocked him. He saw a child given a slave as a present. A slave owner acquaintance he met told him of nailing up a Negro by the ears. This was followed by a severe whipping and the pouring of scalding water onto his naked body. He also heard of a slave owner whipping a Negro woman until she fell down at his feet for dead. When a physician revived her, she was whipped once more while hot sealing wax was dropped onto her. Charles wrote, "It were endless to recount all the shocking instances of diabolical cruelty which these men (as they called themselves) daily practice upon their fellow-creatures; and that on the most trivial occasions."[4] Stark (2003) contended that such events were far too typical among slaves in the English-speaking American colonies as contrasted with much more humane treatment of slaves in the Caribbean where Roman Catholicism was dominant.[5]

John's contact with blacks during a subsequent visit to Charleston was somewhat more benign and spiritual. He preached at a Charleston church and conversed with one of several slaves in attendance. It was the first extended conversation he ever had with a slave. He was amazed to learn that although she lived in a clergyman's home, she was woefully ignorant of the basics of Christianity. Because of inclement weather, Wesley had to return to Georgia on horseback. He conversed with this woman, who accompanied him on this trip, and became acquainted with a slave owner who treated his slaves kindly and who was open to Wesley's interest in providing slaves with confirmation training. He was also able to interest a few other slave owners in implementing such an idea.

John Wesley left America without further contact with slavery, although he began to read publications that heightened his concerns and eventually led to the publication of *Thoughts upon Slavery* some thirty years later. Unfortunately, the moral ideals of the Georgian charter gave way to petitions from landowners to allow slavery. Beginning in 1740 there was lawful slavery in Georgia—a change Wesley noted in a letter after he had become concerned about the inhumanity of slavery, in addition to his concern for the eternal souls of those caught in its throes. He wrote to Anthony Benezet, a French abolitionist, "Mr. Oglethorpe you know went so far as to begin settling a colony without Negroes, but at length the voice of those villains prevailed who sell their country and their God for gold, who laugh at human nature and compassion, and who defy all religion, but that of getting money. It is certainly our duty to do all in our power to check this growing evil. . . . But I fear it will not be stopped till all the kingdoms of the earth become the kingdoms of our God."[6]

It is a sad comment that Wesley's prediction rang true during his lifetime. Wilberforce was only successful in getting Parliament to declare slavery illegal in the British empire during the second decade of the nineteenth century—some twenty years after Wesley's death.

The middle years of the eighteenth century found Wesley consumed with stabilizing the response to his field preaching through local Societies. Overt concern for slaves seemed to be focused on their personal edification and salvation. One very interesting development occurred in the Caribbean through the auspices of Nathaniel Gilbert, who inherited a plantation in Antigua. Gilbert's brother was converted at a Methodist meeting and sent his brother several of Wesley's publications. Wesley's *The Appeals to Men of Reason and Religion* greatly impressed Gilbert. He sought out Wesley when he returned to England. During this visit Wesley baptized two slaves belonging to Gilbert. Upon returning to Antigua, Gilbert began preaching to his slaves, who responded overwhelmingly to his ministrations. Antigua became largely Methodist by the late 1700s. Although emancipation was difficult in those times, Gilbert became a strong foe of slavery and probably introduced to Wesley the thinking of Anthony Benezet—the French Quaker who influenced Wesley to become an ardent abolitionist.

Wesley was always a compulsive reader—both while residing at the Foundery in London and while riding on horseback across all of England, Scotland, Wales, and Ireland. An event in 1772 caused him to begin even more serious reading on the issue of slavery. Lord Chief Justice Mansfield ruled that the American Negro James Somerset came under the general ruling that "whenever and wherever a slave set foot on English soil he was from that moment free."[7] Although a number of jurists argued that this applied to the total empire, the selling of slaves continued in Bristol (English soil) until 1792, and, as previously noted, the House of Commons did not rule slavery illegal until the nineteenth century. But Wesley and many others were stimulated by Mansfield's ruling.

Anthony Benezet became the chief shaper of Wesley's thinking. The Benezet family had sailed from France to Philadelphia in 1731. Although he and his brothers established a successful import business, his real ambition was to be a teacher. During his years as an educator, he became deeply concerned about reports of how slaves were procured and sold. He carried on correspondence with William Wilberforce and other abolitionists. He published pamphlets detailing his opposition to slavery that were distributed free of charge. His 1766 publication of *A Caution and Warning to Great Britain and Her Colonies, in a Short Representation of the Calamitous State of the Enslaved Negroes in British Dominions* went through six editions in America and England. It stressed "the evils of slavery and the inconsistency of the practice with the religion of Christ."[8] Wesley wrote to Benezet after reading some of his pamphlets. Wesley said that he would begin writing about the slave trade in England. This led to Wesley's writing his famous *Thoughts upon Slavery*.

Some have suggested that Wesley's *Thoughts upon Slavery* was but an abridgment of Benezet's *Historical Account of Guinea*, but that is an oversimplification. Only about 30 percent of Wesley's volume is dependent on Benezet. In his traditionally organized and structured manner, Wesley detailed in a masterful way the moral and humanistic arguments against the slave trade. And his publication became the clarion call of the abolitionist movement in Great Britain.

After summarizing the ruling in the Somerset case, Wesley described the conditions in Africa from which slaves were taken. He then demonstrated the brutality of Europeans in capturing and exporting human beings to the New World. After detailing the economic motivation in human slavery, Wesley analyzed this behavior from an ethical and religious point of view. He then argued against the contention that farms in the hot South could be cultivated only by Negroes, who could stand weather that Europeans would find unbearable. He argued persuasively against human trafficking as opposed to the exporting of goods. He concluded that humans are created to be free and have souls destined for eternity.

Thoughts upon Slavery was published in London by Robert Hawes in early 1774 as a pamphlet of fifty-three pages. It sold for a shilling. Wesley sent a copy to Benezet, who republished it in America by that summer. It was soon published in Ireland, followed by publication in Europe. The volume went through thirteen editions over the next thirty years in the United States. In 1787 when the Committee for the Abolition of the Slave Trade was formed, Wesley sent a letter of support to the committee and indicated he would reprint "a large edition of the tract I wrote some years since, *Thoughts upon Slavery*, and send it (which I have an opportunity of doing once a month) to all my friends in Great Britain and Ireland; adding a few words in favour of your design [i.e., the committee], which I believe will have some weight with them. I commend you to Him who is able to carry you through all opposition and support you in all discouragements, and am Gentlemen, Your hearty well-wisher."[9]

This letter of support for the abolition committee was only one of the ways Wesley expressed himself on slavery during these years. In his *Calm Address to Our American Colonies* (1775), he wrote pointedly about the evils of slavery and gave a clear illustration of who was and who was not enslaved, so none of the colonists should mistake his concern. He stated, "You and I, and the English in general, go where we will, and enjoy the fruit of our labours: This is liberty. The Negro does not: This is slavery."[10] Wesley repeated his opinions in *A Serious Address to the People of England, with Regard to the State of the Nation* (1778) and in an article entitled "A Summary View of the Slave Trade" published in the *Arminian Magazine* in 1788. His opposition to slavery was well known among Methodists in America and was reflected in the minutes of conferences in 1780, in which it was stated that the owning of slaves was a cause for expulsion.

Conclusion

Without a doubt, Wesley's letter supporting Wilberforce was noteworthy and worthy of remembering. The great truth, however, is that the letter was but a final testimony to many years of determined concern to rid the world of slavery, this "vilest of human sins."

9

John Wesley the Writer and Publisher

John Wesley published over 370 separate publications. Although Feather, in his *History of British Publishing* (1988), noted that "the largest single category of books produced by British publishers in the eighteenth century was in the field of religion,"[1] he failed to reference Wesley. We may wonder how this could be, considering the prodigious output of this evangelist on horseback. Wesley established a printing house of his own and, at this and other publishing houses, produced original books, abridgments of other writers, extracts of daily journals, tracts, magazines, and letters. As Herbert (1940) commented after surveying all that Wesley wrote, "One begins to realize what an enormous amount of printed matter he caused to be disseminated among English speaking people."[2] In a self-deprecating manner, Wesley wrote, "I have made a little attempt, such as I could consistently with abundance of other employment. Let one that has more leisure and more abilities supply what is here wanting."[3]

Wesley came from a writing family. His father, Samuel, had just finished a commentary on the book of Job when he died. Samuel was also a poet as was John's older brother Samuel Jr., who actually published a volume of poetry. However, the best-known poet of the Wesley family was Charles, John's younger brother. He composed the lyrics to many hymns and was called "the sweet singer of Methodism." Many of Charles's hymns are still sung today.[4]

John Wesley's Diary/Journal

Although he collaborated with Charles in writing some religious poems, John is best known for his narrative writing of an almost-daily journal. The impulse to consistently detail the events of his life in writing was likely due, in part, to the implicit influence of his mother, Suzanna. He adopted her example of living a highly organized life. Initially, this resulted in his following a systematic regime in his studies at Oxford. He outlined books that he read, added comments as he went, and transcribed portions that he wanted to remember. In these endeavors he used a form of shorthand coupled with cipher and abbreviation—a habit that was to serve him well later in his diary and journal.[5]

However, the prompting to actually keep a daily account of his activities came from the reading in 1725 of a recommendation in Jeremy Taylor's *Rules and Exercises for Holy Living and Holy Dying*.[6] Wesley was impressed with Taylor's suggestion that a truly religious man would make a review of his behavior each night before he went to bed. Wesley wrote in his diary, "In reading several parts of this book, I was exceedingly affected: that part in particular which related to purity of intention. Instantly I resolved to dedicate all my life to God, all my thoughts, and words and actions, every part of my life (not some only) must either be a sacrifice to God, or myself, that is, in effect, to the devil."[7]

Thus began his keeping of a diary (and later a journal)—a habit that he faithfully kept from this beginning in 1725 for most of the next sixty-five years before his death in 1791.

Excerpts from the diary included hour-by-hour details of what he was doing and where he went. They even included what he ate and with whom he shared meals. As time went on, Wesley recorded the establishment and activities of the Oxford University Holy Club.

As time went on, the diary changed into a journal that included feelings, judgments, comments, and descriptions of times and places. For example, these writings told of Wesley's weekend romantic exploits, the presentation of his father's book to the queen, and the journey to Georgia as a missionary. In 1739, after he had returned to England from Georgia and gained some notoriety for his leadership of the burgeoning Methodist movement, Wesley was publicly criticized for the way he had handled the Sophie Hopkey affair in Georgia, as described in chapter seven. A "certain Captain Williams," who had himself been in Georgia when Wesley was there, made public statements before the mayor of Bristol that were critical of the circumstances related to Wesley leaving Georgia. To defend himself, Wesley decided to publish his journal account of the affair. Wesley stated in the first extract of his journal:

> I had no design or desire to trouble the world with any of my little affairs; as cannot but appear to every impartial mind, from my having been so long "as one that heareth not;" notwithstanding the loud and frequent calls I have had to answer for myself. Neither should I have done it now, had not Captain Williams's affidavit, published as soon as he had left England, laid an obligation upon me, to do what in me lies, in obedience to that command of God, "Let

not the good which is in you be evil spoken of." With this view I do at length "give an answer to every man that asketh me a reason of the hope which is in me," that in all things "I have a conscience void of offence toward God and toward men."[8]

This first of many journal extracts to follow began with a letter Wesley had sent to a Richard Morgan, the father of a Holy Club member who had committed suicide. It also included an account of the journey to Georgia and his ministry there. This 1739 extract did not fully settle criticism of Wesley, so he published another in 1742. This publishing of journal extracts continued for the rest of his life and became a publication that attained a wide readership. The date of the first entry in the journal extracts was October 14, 1735, and the last entry was October 24, 1790. The extracts themselves were published from 1739 to 1791. They are a virtual autobiography. His accounts of his travels have been described as the best available survey of eighteenth-century England. His journeys to out-of-the-way places and associations with common people filled many readers with eager anticipation to buy the next extract.

A summary of the contents of the journal extracts follows. Each extract is numbered. The basic themes in a given extract are listed, followed by the number of separate entries in a given extract. Each summary ends with the title of a sample entry from the extract.

- First: Wesley as missionary to Georgia; 11 entries; sample entry: "Memorable Atlantic Storm"
- Second: troubles in Georgia, why Wesley returned to England, Peter Bohler; 17 entries; sample entry: "I Felt My Heart Strangely Warmed"
- Third: field preaching, "All the world is my parish," experiences with demons; 13 entries; sample entry: "Yonder Comes Wesley, Galloping"

- Fourth: preaching incidents, Wesley's labor colony, dispute with Whitefield, curious interruptions, the mother of the Wesleys; 25 entries; sample entry: "The Death of Wesley's Mother"
- Fifth: Wesley refused sacraments at Epworth, Cornwall and the Scilly Isles, natural amphitheater at Gwennap; 16 entries; sample entry: "Wesley and the Cock-fighter"
- Sixth: first Methodist conference, press gangs and mobs; 16 entries; sample entry: "Wesley Pushed from a High Wall"
- Seventh: severe weather, Ireland, Wesley's protest against ungodliness; 16 entries; sample entry: "Wesley Dealt with a Mob"
- Eighth: Wesley and the soldiers, in Ireland and Wales again, Wesley burned in effigy, Wesley as an editor; 19 entries; sample entry: "Wesley Rides Ninety Miles"
- Ninth: Wesley's marriage, dealings with Cornwall smugglers, his illness and recovery; 16 entries; sample entry: "Wesley Sleeps in a Cellar"
- Tenth: retirement in Paddington, Wesley slandered, premonitions, a dream; 19 entries; sample entry: "Persecuting the Methodists"
- Eleventh: Wesley—"I do, indeed, live by Preaching," Wesley's advice to travelers, Wesley and the French prisoners; 21 entries; sample entry: "Defeating the Press Gang"
- Twelfth: Wesley's letter to an editor, impositions and declarations, the speaking stature, Wesley's Pentecost; 22 entries; sample entry: "Wesley and the Oatmeal Sellers"

- Thirteen: Wesley in Scotland again, against Methodists' wealth, no law for Methodists, exhausting days, Whitefield; 19 entries; sample entry: "Wesley's Experiment with Lions"
- Fourteenth: justice for Methodists, Methodist character, instructions to parents, Wesley's opinion of Mary, Queen of Scots; 19 entries; sample entry: "Wesley Travels North"
- Fifteenth: Wesley opens a new church, comments on Rosseau, geology, Swedenborg, riding horseback, Gwennap and 20,000 people; 16 entries; sample entry: "Death of Whitefield"
- Sixteenth: Windsor Park, Wesley as autocratic, Glasgow and Perth, at 70 Wesley preaches to 30,000 people; 24 entries; sample entry: "The Earthquake at Madeley"
- Seventeenth: Wesley arrested, a terrible ride, a Methodist Sir Issac Newton, Wesley and the American War; 12 entries; sample entry: "Wesley Criticizes the Scottish Universities"
- Eighteenth: on the Isle of Man, City Road Chapel, Wesley visits Lord George Gordon, 18 entries; sample entry "Wesley Starts a Magazine"
- Nineteenth: an ideal Circuit, Wesley in his 80s, Wesley visits Holland, incidents in Scotland; 21 entries; sample entry: "Remarkable Escape from Prison"
- Twentieth: Wesley collects money for the poor, Wesley visits the House of Lords, his reasons for long life, how is the tide turned; 26 entries; sample entry: "Wesley's Last Hours"[9]

These journal extracts of personal entries that Wesley never intended to be made public became a central part of his publishing ventures and have been as widely studied as his sermons and books. The extracts were the most profitable of all of Wesley's publications. At an early Methodist conference the question was asked, "Should all our Assistants keep journals?" Wesley answered, "By all means, as well for our satisfaction as for the profit of their own souls."[10]

Wesley's Books

The writing of a journal is one thing; the writing of books is another. Journal entries are written a day at a time. Even these are difficult for us to comprehend in a person such as Wesley, who was constantly on the move from one place to another, preaching, advising, and organizing. His days began early and ended late. He may have read as he rode a horse, but he probably did little writing. Books take undisturbed time for reading, thinking, and deliberation. Some explanation of how Wesley wrote books comes from the fact that he spent the winters in London. His travels took place in spring, summer, and fall. Still the output is amazing.

In other chapters we have dealt with books that Wesley wrote out of concerns for healing and slavery. The home health-care manual *Primitive Physick: Or an Easy and Natural Method of Curing Most Diseases* (1747) grew out of Wesley's concern that physicians were expensive and collaborated with apothecaries in prescribing complicated medicines that were ineffective. The application of what Wesley considered God's "secondary cause" in providing free electricity for therapeutic use led him to write *The Desideratum: Or Electricity Made Plain and Useful by a Lover of Mankind and of Common Sense* (1760). His book *Thoughts upon Slavery* (1774) was an expression of concern and compassion for the abuses he saw while in America and his awareness that many of the slave traders were British merchants.

More than once Wesley stated his conviction that "reading Christians will be knowing Christians." So, his overarching goal in books he wrote or edited was to make available literature for the average person and particularly for Methodists. In 1763 he published *A Survey of the Wisdom of God in the Creation: Or a Compendium of Natural Philosophy* in three volumes.[11] The background of this book was based on Wesley's initially negative reaction to the discoveries and teachings of Sir Isaac Newton. Wesley felt that Newton's reliance on the revelation of God in nature might lead people to a distrust of God's revelation in the Bible. Over time, however, Wesley changed his mind. His study of the issues led him to even call Newton a closet Methodist. The volumes in his *Survey* portray nature as a support for the salvation that God offers in the Bible.

In each of the Societies that were organized in the communities where he preached, Wesley established a library and encouraged the reading of good books. He published *The Christian Library* of fifty volumes and recommended that every Methodist Society buy the library and encourage its members to read these books. Each of the books in the *Library* was about three hundred pages long and had a preface and a short biography of the author. Wesley resolved to choose the best among current writers. Some of the writers actually disagreed with Wesley's theological convictions, and this did not bother him. He repeated the old dictum "I think and let think." Herbert noted, "The basis of admission to John Wesley's societies was only by implication an acceptance of any specific doctrines at all. It was rather a certain attitude."[12] What is remarkable is that the idea for a Christian library was expressed to a friend in 1748 and that the last of the fifty volumes in the *Library* came off the press only seven years later, in 1755. Sadly, the idea of a Christian library was not embraced wholeheartedly by the Societies, and the publishing never paid for itself despite Wesley's strong recommendation.

Wesley published a number of other books that were abridgments or extracts of volumes written by others. The copyright laws were not strong, and this was a common practice. These included *The Short Roman History, An Extract from Dr. Cadogan's Dissertation on the Gout and All Chronic Diseases,* and *A Concise Ecclesiastical History, from the Birth of Christ to the Beginning of the Present Century.* Further, in 1753 he published a dictionary because he thought the average reader might be unfamiliar with words in his other publications.

Wesley's *Arminian Magazine*

The final publication to be considered is Wesley's founding of the *Arminian*[13] *Magazine: Consisting of Extracts and Original Treatises on Universal Redemption* in 1778. This does not mean that Wesley wrote nothing else. He wrote over 2,600 letters, several books of hymns, and preached countless sermons—all of which have been published.[14] He wrote numerous pamphlets and tracts of which the first chapter in this book, "The Character of a Methodist," is a reprint of one and *A Calm Address to Our American Colonies* is another.[15]

Wesley noted in 1777 that there were two religious periodicals being published in English: the *Gospel Magazine* and the *Spiritual Magazine*—both of which advocated Calvinism. Both these periodicals had included articles critical of Wesley and his movement. No magazine supportive of the Methodist (Arminian) point of view existed. So, in January 1778 his new publication came off the press. the *Arminian Magazine* promoted Wesley's theology of the possibility of salvation for everyone. It was designed to be fifty to sixty pages that included four parts: "First, a defense of that Grand Christian Doctrine, 'God willeth all men to be saved, and to come to the knowledge of the truth.' Secondly, an extract from the Life of some holy man, whether Lutheran, Church of England, Calvinist, or Arminian. Thirdly, accounts and letters containing the experiences of pious persons, the great part of whom are still alive; and Fourthly, verses explaining or confirming the capital doctrine we have in view."[16]

Wesley warned his detractors, "I have been frequently attacked . . . but I did not answer because we were not on even ground, but that difficulty is now over: whatever they object . . . I can answer in my monthly magazine; and I shall think it my duty so to do when the objection is of some importance."[17] The magazine served two additional purposes: it provided a venue for printing Wesley's sermons as well as for publishing a catalogue of books, pamphlets, and tracts sold by his Methodist Book Concern. At its height, the *Arminian Magazine* had over five thousand subscribers. Continued under the name of the *Wesleyan Methodist Magazine*, Wesley's magazine has the distinction of having the longest record of continuous publication of all religious journals in the world.

Conclusion

This survey of the writing and publishing activity of John Wesley is not meant to be complete in any sense. However, it is complete enough, in my judgment, to leave the reader with the nagging question, How did he do it? Shorthand or not, the amount of published material was prodigious. There was no typewriter or computer to speed the process. Although he lived to be almost eighty-eight, time would have run out on most people before they could have produced over three hundred seventy separate published items—many of which went into more editions and/or revisions. Not all his publishing endeavors were finally successful. But enough of them were so that he could finance a number of his other charitable causes. It was said that when he died he left a few gold coins and the Methodist church. He was a true publishing giant.

10

John Wesley, a Man for All Reasons

John Wesley was truly a remarkable individual. Having been born in 1703 and dying in 1791, he lived in every decade of the eighteenth century. He was a well-known, even famous, individual during his lifetime. The Oxford Story, a long-standing tourist attraction depicting the history of the famous university, featured Wesley as the eighteenth century's most outstanding graduate. Some have conjectured that his ministry to the lower classes was so effective that it saved England from the turmoil that accompanied the French Revolution.

It was not that his message suppressed their frustrations over poverty or their sense of social injustice. No. He identified with their condition. He fought for change. He gave them hope. He inspired them to frugality and cleanliness. He organized them into groups for social support. Above all, his message offered them salvation from their sin.[1]

Wesley's mother, Suzanna, had an early premonition that her son was destined to make a significant contribution in life. It happened when a fire erupted at the parsonage in Epworth, England, where her husband was the priest. John, who was a very young boy, was caught in the second story of the house as the fire spread. There was great concern that he would be killed. A friend braved the fire, rushed up the stairs, grabbed the lad, and pitched him out the window into the outstretched arms of a neighbor. As he was handed to his mother, she was heard to exclaim, "This child is a brand snatched from the burning." From that day on she was convinced that he was saved for a purpose. Her premonition was not in vain.

What can modern Christians glean from the study of Wesley's life? The knowledge of the unique features and accomplishments of a historic Christian leader should not be the main effect of such an endeavor, as interesting as these might be. Were Wesley alive today, he would, no doubt, be very concerned if the facts of his life became the only result of his Christian witness.

Of course, one effect of Wesley's life is the number of denominations that grew out of his tireless work: Wesleyan, African Methodist Episcopal, Free Methodist, Nazarene, and United Methodist. However, in the modern world, denominational designations have paled in their importance. Many people join churches because of family history and have little appreciation for any uniqueness that a denominational label might imply. And most of today's churches combine features from the witness of many historic Christian leaders, and it is difficult to tell whether the average sermon is preached out of one tradition or another. Wesley's life greatly influenced Christendom in general. And this includes Roman Catholicism as well as all Protestant traditions. The compilation of books Wesley recommended to the leaders of his chapels included writings authored by those written long before the Protestant Reformation.

So, what can we learn from Wesley? First, he was very fallible. This trait may sound outlandish since it is not necessarily a feature that lifts up a religious leader's ability to transcend human frailty and meet the trials of life through faith. Wesley's imperfections can be seen clearly in the chapter "John Wesley the Romantic." Here Wesley comes through as thoroughly human—not only in his amorous feelings but also in his timidity, his anger, and his vengeance. He seems like a modern Peter, Jesus' disciple who abandoned his faith under stress. Wesley rationalized his anger toward Sophie Hopkey and used the flimsy excuse that she no longer attended weekly Bible lessons each Wednesday as justification for refusing Holy Communion to her and her new husband. The depression and guilt that he felt as he fled back home to London after this debacle in Savannah make sense to anyone who has ever done something he or she later regretted. These human feelings of guilt and shame in a serious Christian such as Wesley prepared him for the May 24, 1738, prayer meeting during which he felt forgiven for his sins. This gave him the impulse to preach abroad a gospel of personal salvation.

Of course, the events with Sophie Hopkey did not end Wesley's human frailties. His later romantic pursuits further illustrate his giving in to the temptation to lay aside his convictions and act on his emotions in a self-defensive way. We recall how hurt he was when Grace Murray married another man. In a somewhat childish way he pleaded with her, saying that he thought the two of them had a promise to marry one another. Note also how impetuous he was in marrying Molly Vazeille within just a few months after the loss of Grace.

Any hopes that John Wesley would eventually have a happy marriage got shattered quickly. Molly was jealous of his travels from the very beginning of their marriage. She tried traveling with him, but she had no experience riding a horse for long distances, braving inclement weather, sleeping in strange beds, and waiting patiently while Wesley counseled others late into the night. Besides these factors, she was a widow and had children at home. She expressed her emotions loud and clear. She was open and honest with her feelings. Wesley became sanctimonious and cloaked his reaction in pious platitudes about her godly need to fit into his lifestyle. He did not change his habits in the least, and he did not show any deep appreciation for her feelings. They lived separately after 1758. The separation from Molly weighed heavily on him, but he continued his ministry. He accepted the fact that she died and was buried a few days before he was informed. Sadly, this sounds very harsh, and we might wish it had turned out otherwise. He longed for an intimate and committed relationship with a woman, but when it became a reality, he was not able to succeed in it. His brother Charles thought this would happen and had wisely advised Wesley never to marry because of his style of taking long sojourns of preaching away from London.

Although Wesley wrote about each of these romantic endeavors, we never hear him spiritualizing what happened or presuming that they were divine intentions for his life. He grieved. He got angry. He acted impetuously. He rationalized. He protested that he thought God blessed his desires and that he could not understand the outcome. He went on with his mission and lived with the regrets. He was, indeed, a very ordinary man in this regard.

While we might wish Wesley had set a better example in some areas of his life, his perseverance in being a serious Christian is a good example for all believers. The struggle of the Christian life is a lifelong work in progress, and Wesley's experience should provide reassurance that no Christian can live a perfect life. While Wesley encouraged Christians to seek perfection before they died, he never claimed that he had achieved it.

In other areas of his life, Wesley was more confessional about his limitations. Some of his memorable statements attest to his reflections in this regard:

- Once in seven years I burn all my sermons, for it is a shame if I cannot write better sermons now than I did seven years ago.
- The longer I live, the larger allowance I make for human infirmities. I exact more from myself and less from others.
- When I was young, I was sure of everything: in a few years, having been mistaken a thousand times, I was not half so sure of most things as I was before; at present I am hardly sure of anything but what God has revealed to me.
- Though I am always in a haste, I am never in a hurry, because I never undertake more work than I can go through with perfect calmness of spirit.
- We are always open to instruction, willing to be wiser every day than we were before, and to change whatever can change for the better.

A prime facet of his humanness was Wesley's attitude toward his treasured doctrine of perfection. It is very clear that he felt his teachings on the obligation and possibility of Christians becoming perfect in doing the will of God to be the unique essence of what it meant to be a Methodist. Yet Wesley never claimed perfection for himself. He did not call people to look at him as an example of perfection. While he did, indeed, insist that he was trying hard to be perfect, he was very suspicious of any who claimed to have reached perfection. It is noteworthy that the one Bible verse he referenced at the beginning of *The Character of a Methodist* was Philippians 3:12 (KJV): "Not as though I had already attained, either were already perfect: but I follow after, if that I may apprehend that for which also I am apprehended of Christ Jesus."[2]

Another trait of John Wesley seen in this survey of lesser-known facts about his life is *care and concern for others*. This can be vividly seen in the chapters on health care ("John Wesley the Physician"), electricity ("John Wesley the Electrotherapist"), and slavery ("John Wesley the Abolitionist"). Probably, the most famous of his statements illustrates this trait:

> Do all the good you can. By all the means you can. In
> all the ways you can. In all the places you can. At all
> the times you can. To all the people you can. As long
> as ever you can.

He lived out this directive well. It was said that in his lifetime he earned upward of the equivalent of $200,000, but that when he died, he had little if any money, his priestly clothes, and his Bible. He had given all his money away to those in need or spent it on such ventures as books for libraries at his chapels and doctors to provide services in his free health clinics.

The term *enthusiast* was appropriately ascribed to Wesley, as was noted in the introduction. Perhaps a better label would have been *activist*. He was alert to what was happening in the culture around him, and he was willing to get involved. He made statements; he wrote books; he sent letters; he took action; he made attempts to change things for the better. Shortly before he died, the last letter he wrote was to encourage efforts to rid the British empire of the American slave trade.

To understand how different Wesley was from the typical Anglican priest, it is important to remember that he was from the privileged upper class. He was a graduate and, subsequently, a fellow of Oxford University. His ordination included the opportunity to request a "living" (i.e., appointment) to a local parish with an ensured income for life. He had enough stature to request an audience with the queen to present a book on Job his father had written. In full clerical garb he could go anywhere and be honored. He did not need to be concerned with the health of the poor, the wages of workers, the behavior of magistrates, or the plight of slaves. Most Anglican priests were not—at least, openly. They lived lives of privilege apart from such mundane affairs. They did not associate with the lower classes. Wesley did not live the life of the typical Anglican priest. He was an involved activist.

Perhaps the clearest example of Wesley's unique tendency to get involved in caring for others is the story of his perception that static electricity could be used to help people in pain. Through the story of his kite experiment, Benjamin Franklin publicized his discovery that static electricity and stormy lightning were the same. Few people paid attention to this basic conclusion and, instead, became enthralled with the application of static electricity to entertaining demonstrations where sparks would set paper on fire or shoot out the fingers of persons in the dark. Wesley, like other upper-class individuals, was invited to such parlor-evening demonstrations.

But unlike most other upper-class individuals, he bought one of the machines and began to explore its possibilities. He made three observations. One was accidental—he accidentally shocked himself, and the sprain in his foot felt better. He had heard that some doctors were testing the use of "electrifying" (Wesley's term) for relief of pain, and this set his mind wondering to what extent this could be true. The second observation was obvious—the electricity itself cost nothing. Except for the cost of the machine, the electricity was free. The third observation was theological. Wesley reasoned that God intended Franklin to determine that the static rubbing of felt and iron produced an identical force with the lightning in the sky. He reasoned that since God was in the business of alleviating human suffering, he intended humans to discover that they could create a force similar to one he had created naturally via rain and wind. It was God's will that this humanly created force be used to aid recovery from illness. Wesley reasoned that this was one of God's "secondary causes" that God provided in his efforts to bring humanity back from the Adamic fall, which had resulted in pain and death.

Wesley became active in applying this insight to actual healing. In his home health-care manual, *Primitive Physick*, he listed thirty-seven illnesses he felt could be helped or cured by "electrifying" (a shock from the machine). He placed a machine in each of his three free health-care clinics. He called electricity the elixir of life.

It is no accident that churches that bear his name (Wesleyan and/or Methodist) have always been activist organizations. They have sometimes been accused of believing in *works righteousness*, as if they were trying to attain God's righteousness by their good works. Admittedly, this is a danger for all Christians. But where churches are true to John Wesley's understanding of Scripture, they know good works are never a means of salvation but a result of it. John Wesley and his true followers believe strongly in the words of 1 John 4:19: "We love because he first loved us" (NRSV).

A final lesson that Christians can take away after reading this account of lesser-known facts of the life of John Wesley is his *trust in the Bible*. He called himself "a man of one book" (the Bible). Although he read widely and recommended that others follow his example, he still grounded all of his thinking in the Bible. As he stated in *The Character of a Methodist*,

> We believe, indeed, that "all Scripture is given by the inspiration of God;" and herein we are distinguished

from Jews, Turks, and Infidels. We believe the written word of God to be the only and sufficient rule both of Christian faith and practice; and herein we are fundamentally distinguished from those of the Romish Church. . . . But as to all opinions which do not strike at the root of Christianity, we think and let think.

A stronger statement would be hard to find. Wesley wrote these words in the mid-eighteenth century, and much biblical study has gone on since that date. However, it is doubtful that he would change a word in this statement. It contains some convictions that he would consider essential were he alive today.

There are two key words in Wesley's statement that seem to be the core of his convictions: "inspiration" and "written." He had a high view of inspiration. He trusted what had been written. Of course, he knew the Scriptures were human documents, in that human beings wrote them down. He was well versed in church history and knew that the decision of the Patristic Fathers as to which writings would be included was not made overnight but took many years. Wesley made no claim that he knew the process, but he was absolutely convinced that both the process of writing and the process of determining inclusion were God inspired, and he trusted the Bible to be the revealed Word of God in which persons could put their trust.

Wesley also had confidence in what was written—that is, the "words" of Scripture. While he quoted the King James Version of the Bible again and again, he knew that it was a translation and that the original documents were no longer extant. He taught Greek and Hebrew out of the conviction that it was good to get as close as possible to the language used by the inspired writers in order to fathom the meaning of the Scriptures. He wrote commentaries on most of the books of the Bible that could be used by average

Christians to help them understand more deeply what God was communicating through what was written.

Wesley knew that the writers of Scripture were historical figures who had lived in different times and places and sometimes contextualized God's will within the affairs of their days. Wesley knew that the essence of all Scripture was twofold: first, to tell us who God is and what God has done; and second, to tell us what is God's will for daily life. Determining where the written Word reveals God's exact will for all times and where the writer slips in a societal custom that would be considered quaint in another culture, requires discernment and prayer. Wesley saw this in the teaching of Paul that women should have their heads covered in church. He said of this and some parts of the Old Testament, that where a teaching is cultural, ignore it; but where the teaching is revelatory or moral, take it seriously. As he stated in the same paragraph where he discussed inspiration and the written Word, "But as to all opinions which do not strike at the root of Christianity, we think and let think."

I believe that modern Christians might even learn something from John Wesley's deathbed testimony. It is this: that his final verbal witness stands as a natural conclusion to a life dedicated to the renewal of "scriptural holiness" throughout the British Isles and America. The Christian Classics Ethereal Library at Calvin College quotes Methodist Betsie Ritchie's account of Wesley's last day as follows:

> After lying still awhile he called on Mr. Bradford to give him a pen and ink; he brought them, but the right hand had well nigh forgot its cunning, and those active fingers which had been the blessed instruments of spiritual consolation and pleasing instruction to thousands, could no longer perform their office. Some time after, he said to me, "I want to write": I

brought him a pen and ink, and on putting the pen into his hand and holding the paper before him, he said, "I cannot." I replied, "Let me write for you, sir; tell me what you would say." "Nothing," returned he, "but that God is with us." In the forenoon he said, "I will get up." While his things were getting ready, he broke out in a manner which, considering his extreme weakness, astonished us all, in these blessed words: "I'll praise my Maker while I've breath, and when my voice is lost in death, praise shall employ my nobler pow'rs; my days of praise shall ne'er be past, while life, and thought, and being last, or immortality endures."

Truly, John Wesley was a man for all reasons. Although this is a strong claim, very few religious leaders of the last few centuries personify a more constant pursuit of sincere holiness embodied within the foibles of genuine human existence.

Endnotes

Chapter 1: John Wesley the Methodist

1. This is a reference to Philippians 3:12ff. It refers to a central theme in Wesleyan theology, namely, that the Christian life is a process. Implicitly, it refers to the fact that the content to follow, while mentioning characteristics of almost perfect embodiment of God's perfect will, is a statement of aspiration—that is, an ideal to which Methodists aspire throughout their lives.

Chapter 2: John Wesley the Perfectionist

1. It should be noted that others date this as 1741.
2. John Wesley, *A Plain Account of Christian Perfection as Believed and Taught by the Rev. John Wesley, from the Year 1725 to the Year 1777* (New York: Lane & Scott, 1850), 13.
3. Clergymen were those ordained in the Church of England. They were able to administer Holy Communion. Preachers were leaders of Methodist Societies who could preach and teach but not administer the sacraments.
4. Wesley, *A Plain Account*, 48.
5. Ibid., 57.
6. Ibid., 61. This illustrates the dilemma he had in asserting both the power of God to "give" perfection and the "process" that human beings go through in attaining perfection.

7. Ibid., 67.
8. Ibid., 81.
9. Ibid., 80–81.
10. Ibid., 35.
11. Ibid., 42.
12. For further elaboration, see H. N. Malony, "John Wesley, John Calvin, and Martin Luther: An Unholy Triumvirate of Import for Psychology" (Symposium on Wesley as Companion to the Dialogue between Psychology and Theology, Pt. Loma Nazarene University, San Diego, CA., March 28–31, 2001).
13. Wesley, *A Plain Account*, 124.
14. Ibid., 125.
15. Ibid., 96.
16. Ibid., 98.
17. Ibid., 99.
18. Ibid., 100.
19. Ibid., 103–104.
20. Ibid., 89–90.
21. Wesley felt that the extraordinary gifts of the Holy Spirit were common in the early church for the first two or three centuries but were very rare since the time of Constantine.
22. Wesley, *A Plain Account*, 135.
23. W. E. Sangster, *A Path to Perfection: An Examination and Restatement of John Wesley's Doctrine of Christian Perfection* (London: Epworth, 1984), 102–103.
24. Wesley, *A Plain Account*, 145.
25. Ibid.
26. Ibid., 149.
27. Ibid., 138.
28. Ibid., 172.
29. Ibid., 169.

Chapter 3: John Wesley the Organizer

1. D. M. Henderson, *A Model for Making Disciples: John Wesley's Class Meeting* (Nappanee, IN: Evangel Publishing, 1997), 27.
2. Ibid., 28.
3. Ibid.
4. Ibid., 30.
5. Ibid., 44–45.
6. Ibid., 65.
7. Ibid., 71.

8. Ibid.
9. Of course, as the Methodist movement grew, there arose a need for a place for each of the Societies to meet. The Methodist chapel was the answer. The first of these chapels was built by Wesley in the Broadmead section of Bristol in 1739—even before the purchase of the Foundery. Called the New Room, this chapel still exists and is considered a historic heritage site by England. The main floor of wooden pews is surrounded by a wrap-around balcony. A second floor includes a room for conferences and bedrooms for Wesley and other ministers.
10. Henderson, *A Model*, 76.
11. Ibid., 84.
12. John Wesley, *The Journal of the Rev. John Wesley, Vol 1* (New York: E.P. Dutton & Co., 1906), 364.
13. Ibid., 112.
14. Ibid., 115.
15. Ibid., 125.

Chapter 4: John Wesley the Physician

1. This chapter is an adaptation of the article "John Wesley's Primitive Physick: An 18th-century Health Psychology" by H. Newton Malony, which appeared in the *Journal of Health Psychology* 1, no. 2 (1996): 147–159.
2. J. D. Matarazzo, "Behavioral Health's Challenge to Academic, Scientific, and Professional Psychology," *American Psychologist* 37, no. 1 (1982): 4.
3. F. Wilder, *The Remarkable World of John Wesley: Pioneer in Mental Health* (Hicksville, NY: Exposition, 1978), 39–40.
4. C. A. Barager, "John Wesley and Medicine," *Annals of Medical History* 10 (1928): 59.
5. A. W. Hill, *John Wesley among the Physicians: A Study in Eighteenth-Century Medicine* (London: The Epworth Press, 1958), 117.
6. H. Y. Vanderpool, "The Wesleyan-Methodist Tradition," in *Caring and Curing in the Western Religious Traditions*, eds. R. L. Numbers and D. W. Amundsen (New York: Macmillan, 1986), 320.
7. M. L. Edwards, *John Wesley and the 18th Century: A Study of His Social and Political Influence* (London: Allen and Unwin, 1933).
8. W. J. Turrell, *John Wesley: Physician and Electrotherapist* (Oxford: Basil Blackwell, 1938), 16.

9. H. D. Rack, "Doctors, Demons and Early Methodist History," in *The Church and Healing*, ed. W. J. Sheils, *Studies in Church History*, vol. 19 (Oxford, England: Basil Blackwell, 1982), 137–152.
10. W. R. Riddell, "Wesley's System of Medicine," *New York Medical Journal* 99 (1914): 64–68.
11. Hill, *John Wesley among the Physicians*, 15.
12. F. Jeffery, "John Wesley's *Primitive Physick*," *Proceedings of the Wesley Historical Society* 21 (1937): 61.
13. Turrell, *John Wesley: Physician*, 12–13.
14. G. S. Rousseau, "John Wesley's *Primitive Physick*," *Harvard Library Bulletin* 16 (1968).
15. P. W. Ott, "A Corner of History: John Wesley and the Non-naturals," *Preventive Medicine* 9 (1980): 578–584.
16. Barager, "John Wesley and Medicine," 63.
17. John Wesley, "A Plain Account of the People Called Methodists," in *Selections from the Writings of the Reverend John Wesley, M.A.*, ed. Herbert Welch (New York: The Methodist Book Concern, 1918), 193.
18. Vanderpool, "The Wesleyan-Methodist Tradition," 324.
19. Hill, *John Wesley among the Physicians*, 119.
20. Ibid., 121.
21. B. G. Thomas, "John Wesley on the Art of Healing," *American Physician* 32 (1906): 298.
22. Riddell, "Wesley's System of Medicine," 68.
23. Rousseau, "John Wesley's *Primitive Physick*," 245.
24. J. Wesley, *Primitive Physick: Or an Easy and Natural Method of Curing Most Diseases* (London: J. Palmar, 1751), 39.
25. Ibid., 58.
26. Ibid., 71.
27. R. Dunlop, "John Wesley: Medical Missionary to the New World," *Today's Health* 42, no. 12 (1964): 70.
28. Ibid.
29. Wesley, *Primitive Physick*, 47.
30. Hill, *John Wesley among the Physicians*.
31. Hill, *John Wesley among the Physicians*, 22.
32. Wesley, *Primitive Physick*, xx.
33. Ibid.
34. Hill, *John Wesley among the Physicians*, 59–60.
35. Hill, *John Wesley among the Physicians*, 75.
36. Hill, *John Wesley among the Physicians*, 8.
37. S. Ayling, *John Wesley* (London: Collins, 1979), 166.

38. Wesley, *Primitive Physick*, xii–xiii.
39. T. Marriot, "Methodism in Former Days: Medicine and Medical Advice," *Wesleyan Methodist Magazine* 69 (1846): 360.
40. Ibid.
41. Ibid.
42. Dunlop, "John Wesley: Medical Missionary," 23.
43. Barager, "John Wesley and Medicine," 65.

Chapter 5: John Wesley the Electrotherapist
1. This chapter is an adaptation of the article "John Wesley and the Eighteenth Century Therapeutic Uses of Electricity" by H. Newton Malony, which was published in *Perspectives on Science and Christian Faith* 47, no. 4 (1995): 233–254.
2. L. Tyerman, *The Life and Times of Rev. John Wesley, M.A.* (London: Hodder and Stoughton, 1870), 162.
3. F. Schiller, "Reverend Wesley, Doctor Marat and their electrical fire," *Clio Medica*, 15, 159–176.
4. R. A. Hunter, "A Brief Review of the Use of Electricity in Psychiatry with Special Reference to John Wesley," *British Journal of Physical Medicine* 20, no. 5 (1957): 99.
5. J. Wesley, *The Desideratum: Or Electricity Made Plain and Useful by a Lover of Mankind and of Common Sense* (London: Bailliere, Tindall and Cox, 1760), 7, 9.
6. W. D. Hackman, *The History of the Frictional Electrical Machine 1600–1850* (Alphenaan den Rijn: Sizthoff and Noordhoff, 1978).
7. Hunter, "A Brief Review," 100.
8. E. Stainbrook, "The Use of Electricity in Psychiatric Treatment during the Nineteenth Century," *Bulletin of the History of Medicine* 22, no. 2 (1948): 156–177.
9. Hunter, "A Brief Review," 99.
10. A. W. Hill, *John Wesley among the Physicians: A Study in Eighteenth-Century Medicine* (London: The Epworth Press, 1958), 87.
11. F. W. Collier, *John Wesley among the Scientists* (New York: Abingdon Press, 1928), 33–34.
12. Ibid., 133.
13. Hill, *John Wesley among the Physicians*, 105.
14. M. W. Woodward, "Wesley's Electrical Machine," *Nursing Mirror* 114, Supp. 2978 (1962): 10.
15. Wesley, *Desideratum*, 31.
16. Hill, *John Wesley among the Physicians*, 101.

17. R. Dunlop, "John Wesley: Medical Missionary to the New World," *Today's Health* 42, no. 12 (1964): 72.
18. Hill, *John Wesley among the Physicians*, 99.
19. Wesley, *Desideratum*, 3.
20. Ibid., 10.
21. Ibid., 29.
22. Hill, *John Wesley among the Physicians*, 94–95.
23. Wesley, *Desideratum*, 41.
24. Ibid., 42.
25. Ibid., 30, 43, 46, 48, 53, 57, 64, 68.
26. W. J. Turrell, *John Wesley: Physician and Electrotherapist* (Oxford: Basil Blackwell, 1938), 19.
27. Wesley, *Desideratum*, 66.
28. Ibid., 71.
29. Hill, *John Wesley among the Physicians*, 89.
30. Wesley, *Desideratum*, 71–72.
31. Turrell, *John Wesley: Physician*, 7.
32. Hill, *John Wesley among the Physicians*, 92.
33. Ibid., 93.
34. H. Y. Vanderpool, "The Wesleyan-Methodist Tradition," in *Caring and Curing in the Western Religious Traditions*, eds. R. L. Numbers and D. W. Amundsen (New York: Macmillan, 1986), 317–353.
35. Turrell, *John Wesley: Physician*, 24.
36. The following are disorders which Wesley thought benefited from treatment by electrification:

Agues	Fits, Ganglions, Gout, Gravel
Blindness, even from a Gutta Serena	Head Ache
	Hysterics
Blood extravasated	Inflammations
Bronchocele	King's Evil
Chlorosis	Knots in the Flesh
Coldness in the Feet	Lameness, Leprosy
Consumption	Mortification (dead flesh)
Contractions of the Limbs	Pain in the Back, in the Stomach
Cramp	
Deafness, Dropsy	Palpitation of the Heart
Epilepsy	Palsy, Pleurisy
Feet violently disordered	Rheumatism
Felons	Ringworms
Fistula Lacrymalis	St. Anthony's Fire

Sciatica	Tooth-Ache
Shingles	Sprain
Swellings of all Kinds	Surfeit (excessive eating)
Throat sore	Wen (tumour on the scalp,
Toe hurt	goitre)

Chapter 6: John Wesley the Spiritualist

1. J. Wright, *The Epworth Phenomena: To Which Are Appended Certain Psychic Experiences Recorded by John Wesley in the Pages of His Journal* (London: William Rider & Son, Ltd., 1917), 51–59.
2. Ibid., 12.
3. J. Wright suggested that the goblin was clearly a Jacobite who wanted the return of the Stuarts as kings and queens of the British Isles (*Epworth Phenomena*, 10).
4. S. J. Jones, *John Wesley's Conception and Use of Scripture* (Nashville, TN: Kingswood Books, 1995).
5. Bangor Christian Trust, *The Radical Wesley Reconsidered* (London: Olive Tree Press, Ltd., 1984), 51.
6. Ibid., 52.
7. R. P. Heitzenrater, *The Elusive Mr. Wesley: John Wesley as Seen by Contemporaries and Biographers*, vol. 2 (Nashville, TN: Abingdon Press, 1984).

Chapter 7: John Wesley the Romantic

1. M. Bowen, *Wrestling Jacob: A Study of the Life of John Wesley and Some Members of His Family* (London: The Religious Book Club, 1938), 65.
2. Ibid., 67.
3. Ibid., 89.
4. Ibid., 144.
5. Philip Thicknesse, a youth who accompanied Sophie Hopkey to church in Savannah, wrote an anonymous letter to the *Gentleman's Magazine* shortly after Wesley's death in 1791, noting that only young women were invited to Wesley's house after worship. He wrote, "I well remember wondering why I was not asked also. Surely, said I, my soul is as of much importance as theirs." See R. P. Heinzenrater, *The Elusive Mr. Wesley: John Wesley as Seen by Contemporaries and Biographers*, vol. 2 (Nashville, TN: Abingdon Press, 1984), 59.
6. S. Ayling, *John Wesley* (New York: Collins, 1979), 75.
7. Bowen, *Wrestling Jacob*, 165.

8. H. Abelove, *The Evangelist of Desire: John Wesley and the Methodists* (Stanford, CA: Stanford University Press, 1990), 49.

9. Abelove cited a fascinating quote from Wesley's 1765 pamphlet: Single people "were 'exempt' from 'the numberless Occasions of Sorrow and Anxiety with which Heads of Families are intangled: Especially those, who have sickly, or unhappy, or disobedient children.'" Servants, Wesley explained, could be fired if they proved unsatisfactory. But children, even when bad or unhealthy, remained as permanent encumbrance to their parents. This encumbrance single people escaped (*Evangelist of Desire*, 52).

10. Bowen, *Wrestling Jacob*, 279.

11. Abelove, *Evangelist of Desire*, 57.

12. Bowen, *Wrestling Jacob*, 284.

13. Ibid., 285.

14. Ayling, *John Wesley*, 214.

15. Ibid., 215.

16. J. Singleton, *At the Roots of Methodism: Marriage Revealed Wesley's Own Humanity* (Nashville, TN: United Methodist News Service), 2. The website was accessed Februry 2009 but is currently (April 2010) being updated: <http://www.umc.org/umns/98/nov/670t.htm>.

17. Ibid.

18. Ibid.

Chapter 8: John Wesley the Abolitionist

1. W. T. Smith, *John Wesley and Slavery* (Nashville, TN: Abingdon Press, 1986), 117.

2. Ibid., 118.

3. Ibid., 36.

4. Ibid., 42.

5. R. Stark, *For the Glory of God: How Monotheism Led to Reformations, Science, Witch-hunts, and the End of Slavery* (Princeton, NJ: Princeton University Press, 2003).

6. Smith, *John Wesley and Slavery*, 53.

7. Ibid., 76.

8. Ibid., 80.

9. Ibid., 107.

10. Ibid., 102.

Chapter 9: John Wesley the Writer and Publisher

1. J. Feather, *A History of British Publishing* (London: Routledge, 1988), 96.

2. T. W. Herbert, *John Wesley as Editor and Publisher* (Princeton, NJ: Princeton University Press, 1940), 121.

3. Ibid., 122.

4. Examples of familiar Charles Wesley hymns are "O for a Thousand Tongues to Sing," "Jesus, Lover of My Soul," "A Charge to Keep I Have," "Love Divine, All Love Excelling," "All Praise to Our Redeeming Lord," "And Are We Yet Alive," "Come, Thou Long-Expected Jesus," "Hark! the Herald Angels Sing," and "Christ the Lord Is Risen Today." An examination of one hymnal found sixty-four hymns written by Charles—far more than any other author.

5. Wesley used the abbreviations below. This code was eventually deciphered by Rev. N. Curnock. When the extracts were published, Wesley translated his notes into English, of course.

Z2W4K2	HT2	P1N	Y45QX
HTK4F	HT2	K4HH2N	2VVJ
J4P24N2	YQ1MM2X	T3J	T1NXJ
4G2K	HT2	P1N'J	M4YR2HJ
K2Q2IJ3NV	1N	1FW5Q	JP2QQ
3NJ3X2	HT2	P1N'J	YQ4HT2J.

Code						
A	B	C	D	E	F	G
1	Z	Y	X	2	W	V
H	I	J	K	L	M	N
T	3	S	R	Q	P	N
O	P	Q	R	S	T	U
4	M	L	K	J	H	5
V	W	X	Y	Z		
G	F	D	C	B		

Reprinted from: http://www.request.org.uk/main/history/georgians/wesley/wesley03.htm.

6. The recommendation to read Taylor's book actually came from Betty Kirkham in whose home Wesley visited frequently. She was probably the first woman for whom Wesley had romantic feelings.

7. John Wesley, *A Plain Account of Christian Perfection as Believed and Taught by the Rev. John Wesley, from the Year 1725 to the Year 1777* (New York: Lane & Scott, 1850), 4.
8. P. L. Parker, ed., *The Journal of John Wesley* (Chicago: Moody Press, 1951), 2.
9. Adapted from the table of contents of P. L. Parker, ed., *The Journal of John Wesley* (Chicago: Moody Press, 1951).
10. Herbert, *John Wesley as Editor*, 13.
11. These three volumes had grown to five volumes in a later edition of 1777.
12. Herbert, *John Wesley as Editor*, 32.
13. Jacob Arminius, for whom the magazine was named, was a theologian in the 16th century who objected to three of the five points of Calvinism: (1) unconditional election, (2) limited atonement, and (3) irresistible grace. He revised a fourth point (perseverance of the saints) and modified a fifth (total depravity). Wesley and many others were influenced by his thinking and considered themselves Arminian.
14. *Sermons on Several Occasions* and *Sacred Melody: Or a Choice Collection of Psalm and Hymn Tunes, with a Short Introduction* are examples.
15. Wesley was convinced the colonists were committing grave error in seeking independence. He was strongly supportive of the monarchy.
16. Herbert, *John Wesley as Editor*, 34.
17. Ibid., 36.

Chapter 10: John Wesley, a Man for All Reasons

1. Wesley organized credit unions from which persons could borrow money. He established Kingswood School for children. He spoke out against poor wages for potters in Stoke-on-Trent and against smuggling by the citizens of Penzance. Some of his sayings are memorable: "Cleanliness is next to godliness"; "The Bible knows nothing about solitary religion"; "Make all you can, save all you can, give all you can"; "The best of it is, God is with us."
2. Christians today might understand this verse better as "Not that I have already obtained this or have already reached the goal; but I press on to make it my own, because Christ Jesus has made me his own" (NRSV).

James Carter

Stanley Easton